# NOTES OF SOME WANDERINGS
WITH THE SWAMI VIVEKANANDA

# NOTES OF SOME WANDERINGS
## WITH THE SWAMI VIVEKANANDA

BY

**SISTER NIVEDITA**

GYAN

*Published by*

GYAN

Gyan Publishing House
5, Ansari Road
Daryaganj, New Delhi-110002
Phone: 011-47034999, 9811692060
E-mail: books@gyanbooks.com

*Distribution Network*
gyanbooks.com
India, USA, Canada, UK, Australia



ISBN: 978-81-212-1050-8 (HB)
First Published, 1913

2nd Impression 2024

*Printed at:* Gyan Press, Delhi.



**NOTES OF SOME WANDERINGS WITH THE SWAMI VIVEKANANDA**
Author: SISTER NIVEDITA

# Notes of some Wanderings
## WITH THE SWAMI VIVEKANANDA
BY SISTER NIVEDITA OF
RAMAKRISHNA-VIVEKANANDA

*Author of "The Web of Indian Life";
"The Civic and National Ideals";
"Cradle-Tales of Hinduism";
"The Master as I saw Him"
etc., etc.*

CALCUTTA:
UDBODHAN OFFICE,
*1, Mukherjee Lane, Baghbazar,*
1922.

# CONTENTS.

## FOREWORD.



## CHAPTER I

### THE HOME ON THE GANGES.

# CHAPTER II

## AT NAINITAL AND ALMORA.



# CHAPTER III

## MORNING TALKS AT ALMORA.

## CHAPTER V

### ON THE WAY TO BARAMULLA.



## CHAPTER VI

### THE VALE OF KASHMIR.



## CHAPTER VII

### LIFE AT SRINAGAR.

# CHAPTER VIII

## THE TEMPLE OF PANDRENTHAN.

## CHAPTER IX

### WALKS AND TALKS BESIDE THE JHELLUM.



## CHAPTER X

### THE SHRINE OF AMARNATH.

## CHAPTER XI

### AT SRINAGAR ON THE RETURN JOURNEY.



## CHAPTER XII

### THE CAMP UNDER THE CHENNAARS.

---

Jaya Dhiramata Swamiji Nivedita

# FOREWARD

*Persons* :—The Swami Vivekananda ; Guru-bhais ; and disciples.
A party of European guests and disciples, amongst whom were Dhirâ Mâtâ, the Steady Mother ; One whose name was Jayâ ; and Niveditâ.
*Place* :—Different parts of India.
*Time* :—The year 1898.

Beautiful have been the days of this year. In them the Ideal has become the Real. First in our river-side cottage at Belur; then in the Himalayas, at Naini-Tal and Almora; afterwards wandering here and there through Kashmir;—everywhere have come hours never to be forgotten, words that will echo through our lives for ever, and once at least, a glimpse of the Beatific Vision.

It has been all play.

We have seen a love that would be one with the humblest and most ignorant, seeing the world for the moment through his eyes, as if criticism were not; we have laughed over the colossal caprice of genius; we have warmed ourselves at heroic fires; and we have been present, as it were, at the awakening of the Holy child.

But there has been nothing grim or serious about any of these things. Pain has come close to all of us. Solemn anniversaries have been and gone. But sorrow was lifted into a golden light, where it was made radiant, and did not destroy.

Fain, if I could, would I describe our journeys. Even as I write I see the irises in bloom at Baramulla; the young rice beneath the poplars at Islamabad; starlight scenes in Himalayan forests; and the royal beauties of Delhi and the Taj. One longs to attempt some memorial of these. It would be worse than useless. Not, then, in words, but in the light of memory, they are enshrined for ever, together with the kindly and gentle folk who dwell among them, and whom we trust always to have left the gladder for our coming.

We have learnt something of the mood in which new faiths are born, and of the Persons who inspire such faiths. For we have been with one who drew all men to him,—listening to all, feeling with all, and refusing none. We have known a humility that wiped out all littleness, a renunciation that would die for scorn of oppression and pity of the oppressed, a love that would bless even the oncoming feet of torture and of death. We have joined hands with that woman who washed the feet of the Lord with her tears, and wiped them with the hairs of her head. We have lacked, not the occasion, but her passionate unconsciousness of self.

Seated under a tree in the garden of dead emperors there came to us a vision of all the rich and splendid things of Earth, offering themselves as a shrine for the great of soul. The storied windows of cathedrals, and the jewelled thrones of kings, the banners of great captains and the vestments of the priests, the pageants of cities, and the retreats of the proud,—all came, and all were rejected.

In the garments of the beggar, despised by the alien, worshipped by the people, we have seen him ; and only the bread of toil, the shelter of cottage-roofs, and the common road across the cornfields seem real enough for the back ground to this life...............Amongst his own, the ignorant loved him as much as scholars and statesmen. The boatmen watched the river, in his absence, for his return, and servants disputed with guests to do him service. And through it all, the veil of playfulness was never dropped. "They played with the Lord," and instinctively they knew it.

To those who have known such hours, life is richer and sweeter, and in the long nights even the wind in the palm-trees seems to cry—

"Mahâdeva ! Mahâdeva ! Mahâdeva !"

# CHAPTER I

## THE HOUSE ON THE GANGES.

*Place* :—A cottage at Belur, besides the Ganges.
*Time* :—March to May 11th.

Of the home by the Ganges, the Master had said to one "You will find that little house of Dhirâ Mâtâ like heaven, for it is all love, from beginning to end."

It was so indeed. Within, an unbroken harmony, and without, everything alike beautiful,—the green stretch of grass, the tall cocoanut palms, the little brown villages in the jungle, and the *nilkantha* that built her nest in a tree-top beside us, on purpose to bring us the blessings of Siva. In the morning the shadows lay behind the house: but in the afternoons we could sit in front, worshipping the Ganges herself,—great leonine mother !—and in sight of Dakshineswar.

There came one and another with traditions of the past; and we learnt of the Master's eight year's wanderings; of the name changed from village to village; of the *Nirvikalpa Samâdhi;* and of that sacred sorrow, too deep for words, or for common sight, that one who loved had alone seen. And there, too, came the Master Himself, with his stories of Umâ and Siva, of Râdhâ and Krishna, and his fragments of song and poetry.

It seemed as if he knew that the first material of a new consciousness must be a succession of vivid, but isolated experiences, poured out without proper sequence, so as to provoke the mind of the learner to work for its own conception of order and relation. At any rate, whether he knew it or not, this was the canon of educational science that he unconsciously fulfilled. For the most part, it was the Indian religions that he portrayed for us, to-day dealing with one, and to-morrow with another, his choice guided, seemingly, by the whim of the moment. But it was not religion only that he poured out upon us. Sometimes it would be history. Again, it would be folk-lore. On still another occasion, it would be the manifold anomalies and inconsistencies of race, caste, and custom. In fact India herself became, as heard in him, as the last and noblest of the *Pûrânas*, uttering itself through his lips.

Another point in which he had caught a great psychological secret was that of never trying to soften for us that which would at first sight be difficult or repellent. In matters Indian he would rather put forward, in its extreme form, at the beginning of our experience, all that it might seem impossible for European minds to enjoy. Thus he would quote, for instance, some verse about Gouri and Sankar in a single form—

"On one side grows the hair in long black curls,
And on the other, corded like rope.
On one side are seen the beautiful garlands,
On the other, bone earrings and snake-like coils.
One side is white with ashes, like the snow mountains,
The other, golden as the light of dawn.
For He, the Lord, took a form,

And that was a divided form,
Half-woman and half-man."

And carried by his burning enthusiasm it was possible to enter into these things, and dimly, even then, to apprehend their meaning.

Whatever might be the subject of the conversation, it ended always on the note of the Infinite. Indeed I do not know that our Master's realisation of the Adwaita Philosophy has been in anything more convincing than in this matter of his interpretation of the world. He might appear to take up any subject, literary, ethnological, or scientific, but he always made us feel it as an illustration of the Ultimate Vision. There was, for him, nothing secular. He had a loathing for bondage, and a horror of those who "cover chains with flowers," but he never failed to make the true critic's distinction between this and the highest forms of art. One day we were receiving European guests, and he entered into a long talk about Persian poetry. Then suddenly, finding himself quoting the poem that says, "For one mole on the face of my Beloved, I would give all the wealth of Samarcand!" he turned and said energetically

"I would not give a straw, you know, for the man who was incapable of appreciating a love song!" His talk, too teemed with epigrams. It was that same afternoon, in the course of a long political argument, that he said "In order to become a nation, it appears that *we need a common hate* as well as a common love."

Several months later he remarked that before one who had a mission he never talked of any of the gods save Umâ and Siva. For Siva and the Mother made the great workers. Yet I have sometimes wondered if he knew at this time how the end of every theme was *bhakti*. Much as he dreaded the luxury of spiritual emotion for those who might be enervated by it, he could not help giving glimpses of what it meant to be consumed with the intoxication of God. And so he would chant for us such poems as—

"They have made Râdhâ queen, in the beautiful groves of Brindâban.
At her gate stands Krishna, on guard.
His flute is singing all the time:
'Râdhâ is about to distribute infinite wealth of love.

Though I am guard, all the world may
enter.
Come all ye who thirst ! Say only 'Glory
unto Râdhâ !'
Enter the region of love !"

Or he would give us the great antiphonal Chorus of the Cowherds, written by his friend :*

*Men.* 'Thou art the Soul of souls,
Thou yellow garbed,
With thy blue eyes.

*Women.* Thou dark One ! Thou
Shepherd of Brindâban !
Kneeling at the feet of the
Sheperdesses.

*Men.* My soul sing the praise of
the glory of the Lord,
Who took the human form.

*Women.* Thy beauty for us, the
Gopis.

*Men.* Thou Lord of Sacrifice.
Saviour of the weak.

---

* The late Bengali dramatist, Babu Girish Chandra Ghose.

*Women.* Who lovest Râdhâ, and thy body floats on its own tears.'

One such day (May, 9) we can never forget. We had been sitting talking under the trees, when suddenly a storm came on. We moved to the terrace, overhanging the river, and then to the verandah. Not a moment too soon. Within ten minutes, the opposite bank of the Ganges was hidden from our view, and in the blackness before us we could hear the rain falling in torrents, and the thunder crashing, while every now and then there was a lurid flash of lightning.

And yet, amidst all the turmoil of the elements, we sat on, in our little verandah, absorbed in a drama far more intense. One form passed back and forth across our tiny stage; one voice compassed all the players; and the play that was acted before us was the love of the soul for God!...........Till we, too caught the kindling, and loved for the moment with a fire that the rushing river could not put out nor the hurricane disturb. "Shall many, waters quench Love, or the floods overwhelm it?" And before Prometheus left us, we knelt before him together and he blest us all.

*May, 17.*

One day, early in the cottage-life, the Swami took the Dhirâ Mâtâ, and her whose name was Jayâ, to be received for the first time by Sâradâ Devi, who had come from her village home, to Calcutta, at his call. Thence they brought back with them for a few hours, a guest to whom the memory of that day makes one of life's great festivals. Never can she forget the fragrance of the Ganges, nor the long talk with the Master, nor the service Jayâ had done that morning by winning the most orthodox of Hindu woman to eat with her foreign disciples; nor any one of the many happy ties that that day brought into existence and consecrated.

*March, 25.*

A week later the same guest was there again, coming late on Wednesday, and going away on Saturday evening. At this time, the Swami kept the custom of coming to the cottage early, and spending the morning-hours there, and again returning in the late afternoon. On the second morning of this visit, however,—Friday, the Christian feast of the Annunciation,—he took us all three back to the Math, and there, in the worship-room, was held a little service of initiation, where one was made a Brahmachârini. That was the happiest of mornings. After the service, we were taken upstairs. The Swami put on the ashes and bone-earrings and matted locks of a Siva-yogi, and sang and played to us—Indian music on Indian instruments,—for an hour.

And in the evening, in our boat on the Ganges, he opened his heart to us, and told us much of his questions and anxieties regarding the trust that he held from his own Master.

Another week, and he was gone to Darjeeling, and till the day that the plague declaration brought him back we saw him again no more.

*May, 3.*

Then two of us met him in the house of our Holy Mother. The political sky was black.

It seemed as if a storm were about to burst. The moon of those evenings had the brown haze about it that is said to betoken civil disturbance—and already plague, panic, and riot were doing their fell work. And the Master turned to the two and said, "There are some who scoff at the existence of Kâli. Yet to-day She is out there amongst the people. They are frantic with fear, and the soldiery have been called to deal out death. Who can say that God does not manifest Himself as Evil as well as Good? But only the Hindu dares to worship Him in the evil."

He had come back, and the old life was resumed once more, as far as could be, seeing that an epidemic was in prospect, and that measures were on hand to give the people confidence. As long as this possibility darkened the horizon, he would not leave Calcutta. But it passed away, and those happy days with it, and the time came that we should go.

# CHAPTER II

## AT NAINI TAL AND ALMORA

*Persons* :—The Swami Vivekananda ; Guru-bhâis*, and disciples.
A party of Europeans, amongst whom were Dhirâ Mâtâ, the 'Steady Mother ;' 'One whose name was Jayâ'; and Niveditâ.
*Place* :—The Himalayas.
*Time* :—May 11 to May 25, 1898.

We were a large party, or, indeed, two parties, that left Howrah station on Wednesday evening, and on Friday morning came in sight of the Himalayas. They seemed to rise suddenly out of the plains, a few hundred yards away.

Naini Tal was made beautiful by three things,—the Master's pleasure in introducing to us his disciple, the Râjâ of Khetri; the dancing girls who met us and asked us where to find him,

* Spiritual brethren ; disciples of one and the same Master are so called.

and were received by him, inspite of the remonstrances of others; and by the Mohammedan gentleman who said "Swamiji, if in after-times any claim you as an avatâr, an especial incarnation of the Deity—remember that I, a Mohammedan, am the first!"

It was here, too, that we heard a long talk on Ram Mohun Roy, in which he pointed out three things as the dominant notes of this teacher's message, his acceptance of the Vedanta, his preaching of patriotism, and the love that embraced the Mussulman equally with the Hindu. In all these things, he claimed himself to have taken up the task that the breadth and foresight of Ram Mohun Roy had mapped out.

The incident of the dancing girls occurred in consequence of our visit to the two temples at the head of the tarn, which from time immemorial have been places of pilgrimage, making the beautiful little "Eye Lake" holy. Here, offering worship, we found two nautch-women. When they had finished, they came up to us, and we in broken language, entered into conversation with them. We took them for respectable ladies of the town, and were much astonished, later, at the storm which had evidently passed over the Swami's audience at his refusal to have them turned away. Am I mistaken in thinking that it was in connection with these dancing-women of Naini Tal that he first told us the story, many times repeated, of the nautch-girl of Khetri? He had been angry at the invitation to see her, but being prevailed upon to come, she sang—

"O Lord, look not upon my evil qualities!
Thy name, O Lord, is Same-Sightedness,
Make us both the same Brahman!

One piece of iron is the knife in the hand of the butcher
And another piece of iron is the image in the temple.
But when they touch the philosopher's stone,
Both alike turn to gold!

One drop of water is in the sacred Jumna,
And one is foul in a ditch by the roadside.
But when they fall into the Ganges,
Both alike become holy!

So, Lord, look not upon my evil qualities !
Thy name, O Lord, is Same-Sightedness.
Make us both the same Brahman !"

And then, said the Master of himself, the scales fell from his eyes, and seeing that all are indeed one, he condemned no more. [And she whose name is Jayâ, heard from another of this same visit, when to the assembled women he spoke words of power that moved all hearts,—full of love and tenderness, without separation and without reproach.]

It was late in the afternoon when we left Naini Tal for Almora, and night overtook us while still travelling through the forest. On and on we went, following the road into deep gullies, and out again, round the shoulders of projecting hill sides, always under the shadow of great trees, and always preceded by torches and lanterns to keep off bears and tigers. While day lasted we had seen the "rose-forests" and the maiden-hair fern by the spring sides, and the scarlet blossoms on the wild pomegranate bushes; but with nightfall, only the fragrance of these and the honeysuckles was left to us, and we journeyed on, content to know nothing, save silence and starlight, and the grandeur of the mountains—till we reached a quaintly placed dak-bungalow, on the mountain side, in the midst of trees. There after sometime, Swamiji arrived with his party, full of fun, and keen in his appreciation of everything that concerned the comfort of his guests, but full before all, of the poetry of the weird "night scenes" without, the coolies by their fires, and the neighing horses, the Poor Man's Shelter near, and the whispering trees and solemn blackness of the forest.

From the day that we arrived at Almora the Swami renewed his habit of coming over to us at our early breakfast, and spending some hours in talk. Then and always, he was an exceedingly light sleeper, and I imagine that his visit to us, early as the hour might be, was often paid during the course of his return with his monks from a still earlier walk. Sometimes, but rarely, we saw him again in the evening, either meeting him when out for a walk, or going ourselves to Capt. Sevier's where he and his party were staying, and seeing him there. And once he came at that time to call on us.

Into these morning talks at Almora, a strange new element, painful but salutary to remember, had crept. There appeared to be, on one side, a curious bitterness and distrust, and, on the other, irritation and defiance. The youngest of the Swami's disciples at this time, it must be remembered, was an English woman, and of how much this fact meant intellectually,—what a strong bias it implied, and always does imply, in the reading of India, what an idealism of the English race and all their deeds and history,—the Swami himself had had no conception till the day after her initiation at the monastery. Then he had asked her some exultant question, as to which nation she now belonged to, and had been startled to find with what a passion of loyalty and worship she regarded the English flag, giving to it much of the feeling that an Indian woman would give to her *Thakoor*. His surprise and disappointment at the moment were scarcely perceptible. A startled look, no more. Nor did his discovery of the superficial way in which this disciple had joined herself with his people in any degree affect his confidence and courtesy during the remaining weeks spent in the plains. But with Almora, it seemed as if a going-to-school, had commenced, and just as schooling is often disagreeable to the taught, so here, though it cost infinite pain, the blindness of a half-view must be done away. A mind must be brought to change its centre of gravity. It was never more than this; never the dictating of opinion or creed; never more than emancipation from partiality. Even at the end of the terrible experience, when this method, as regarded race and country, was renounced, never to be taken up systematically again, the Swami did not call for any confession of faith, any declaration of new opinion. He dropped the whole question. His listener went free. But he had revealed a different standpoint in thought and feeling, so completely and so strongly as to make it impossible for her to rest, until later, by her own labours, she had arrived at a view in which both these partial presentments stood rationalised and accounted for "Really, patriotism like yours is sin!" He exclaimed once, many weeks later, when the process of obtaining an uncoloured judgment on some incident had been more than commonly exasperating. "All that I want you to see is that most people's actions are the expression of self-interest, and you constantly oppose to this the idea that a certain race are all angels. Ignorance so determined is wickedness!" Another question on which this same disciple showed a most bitter obstinacy was that of the current western estimate of woman. Both these limitations of her sympathy look petty and vulgar enough to her now, as compared with the open and disinterested attitude of the mind that welcomes truth. But at the time they were a veritable lion in the path, and remained so until she had grasped the folly of allowing anything whatever to obscure to her the personality that was here revealing itself. Once having seen this, it was easy to be passive to those things that could not be accepted, or could not be understood, and to leave to time the formation of ultimate judgments regarding them. In every case it had been some ideal of the past that had raised a barrier to the movement of her sympathy, and surely it is always so. It is the worships of one era which forge the fetters of the next.

These morning talks at Almora then, took the form of assults upon deep-rooted preconceptions, social, literary, and artistic, or of long comparisons of Indian and European history and sentiments, often containing extended observations of very great value. One characteristic of the Swami was the habit of attacking the absues of a country or society openly and vigorously when he was in its midst, whereas after he had left it, it would often seem as if nothing but its virtues were remembered by him. He was always testing his disciples, and the manner of these particular discourses was probably adopted in order to put to the proof the courage and sincerity of one who was both woman and European.

# CHAPTER III

## MORNING TALKS AT ALMORA

*Place* :—Almora.
*Time* :—May and June 1898.

The first morning, the talk was that of the central ideals of civilization,—in the West, truth, in the East, chastity. He justified Hindu marriage-customs, as springing from the pursuit of this ideal, and from the woman's need of protection, in combination. And he traced out the relation of the whole subject to the Philosophy of the Absolute.

Another morning he began by observing that as there were four main castes,—Brâhman, Kshattriya, Bunea, Sudra,—so there were four great national functions, the religious or priestly, fulfilled by the Hindus, the military, by the Roman Empire; the mercantile by England today; and the democratic by America in the future. And here he lunched off into a glowing prophetic forecast of how America would yet solve the problems of the Sudra,—the problems of freedom and co-operation,—and turned to relate to a non-American listener, the generosity of the arrangements which that people had attempted to make for their aborigines.

Again it would be an eager *résumé* of the history of India or of the Moguls whose greatness never wearied him. Every now and then, throughout the summer, he would break out into descriptions of Delhi and Agra. Once he described the Taj as "a dimness, and again a dimness, and there—a grave!" Another time, he spoke of Shah Jehan, and then, with a burst of enthusiasm,—"Ah! *He* was the glory of his line! A feeling for, and discrimination of beauty that are unparalled in history. And an artist himself! I have seen a manuscript illuminated by him, which is one of the art-treasures of India. What a genius!" Oftener still, it was Akbar of whom he would tell, almost with tears in his voice, and a passion easier to understand, beside that undomed tomb, open to sun and wind, the grave of Secundra at Agra.

But all the more universal forms of human

feeling were open to the Master. In one mood he talked of China as if she were the treasure-house of the world, and told us of the thrill with which he saw inscriptions in old Bengali (Kutil?) characters, over the doors of Chinese temples. Few things could be more eloquent of the vagueness of Western ideas regarding Oriental peoples than the fact that one of his listeners alleged untruthfulness as a notorious quality of that race. As a matter of fact the Chinese are famous in the United States, where they are known as business-men, for their remarkable commercial integrity, developed to a point far beyond that of the Western requirement of the written word. So the objection was an instance of misrepresentation, which, though disgraceful, is nevertheless too common. But in any case the Swami would have none of it. Untruthfulness! Social rigidity! What were these, except very, very relative terms? And as to untruthfulness in particular, could commercial life, or social life, or any other form of co-operation go on for a day, if men did not trust men? Untruthfulness as a necessity of etiquette? And how was that different from the Western idea? Is the Englishman always glad and always sorry at the proper place? But there is still a difference of degree? Perhaps—but only of degree!

Or he might wander as far afield as Italy, that "greatest of the countries of Europe, land of religion and of art; alike of imperial organization and of Mazzini;—mother of ideas, of culture, and of freedom!"

One day it was Sivaji and the Mahrattas and the year's wandering as a *Sannyâsi*, that won him home to Raigarh. "And to this day," said the Swami, "authority in India dreads the *Sannyâsi*, lest he conceal beneath his yellow garb another Sivâji."

Often the enquiry, Who and what are the Aryans?—absorbed his attention; and, holding that their origin was complex, he would tell us how in Switzerland he had felt himself to be in China, so like were the types. He believed too that the same was true of some parts of Norway. Then there were scraps of information about countries and physiognomies, an impassioned tale of the Hungarian scholar, who traced the Huns to Tibet, and lies buried in Darjeeling and so on.

It was very interesting throughout this summer, to watch,—not only in the Swami's case, but in that of all persons who might be regarded as representative of the old Indian culture,—how strong was the fascination exerted by enquiries of this nature. It seemed as if in the intellectual life of the East, questions of race and custom and ethnological origins and potentialities took the place that the observation of international politics might hold in the West. The idea suggested itself that Oriental scholars and statesmen could never ignore this element in their peculiar problems, and would be likely at the same time to bring a very valuable power of discrimination to bear upon it.

Sometimes the Swami would deal with the rift between Brahmins and Kshattriyas, painting the whole history of India as a struggle between the two, and showing that the latter had always embodied the rising, fetter-destroying impulses of the nation. He could give excellent reason too for the faith that was in him that the Kayasthas of modern Bengal represented the pre-

Mauryan Kshattriyas. He would portary the two opposing types of culture, the one classical, intensive, and saturated with an ever-deepening sense of tradition and custom; the other, defiant, impulsive, and liberal in its out-look. It was part of a deep-lying law of the historic development that Rama, Krishna, and Buddha had all arisen in the kingly, and not in the priestly caste. And in this paradoxical moment, Buddhism was reduced to a caste-smashing formula—"a religion invented by the Kshattriyas" as a crushing rejoineder to Brahminism!

That was a great hour indeed, when he spoke of Buddha; for, catching a word that seemed to identify him with its anti-Brahminical spirit, an uncomprehending listener said, "Why Swami, I did not know that you were a Buddhist!" "Madam," he said rounding on her, his whole face aglow with the inspiration of that name, "I am the servant of the servants of the servants of Buddha. Who was there ever like Him?—the Lord—who never performed one action for Himself—with a heart that embraced the whole world! So full of pity that He—prince and monk—would give His life to save a little goat! So loving that He sacrificed himself to the hunger of a tigress!—to the hospitality of a pariah and blessed him! And He came into my room when I was a boy and I fell at His feet! For I knew it was the Lord Himself!"

Many times he spoke of Buddha in this fashion, sometimes at Belur and sometimes afterwards. And once he told us the story of Ambâpâli, the beautiful courtesan who feasted Him in words that re-called the revolt of Rossetti's great half-sonnet of Mary Magdalene:—

"Oh loose me! Seest thou not my Bridegroom's face,
That draws me to him? For his feet my kiss,
My hair, my tears, He craves to-day:—And oh!
What words can tell what other day and place
Shall see me clasp those blood-stained feet of His?
He needs me, calls me, loves me, let me go!"

But national feeling did not have it all its own way. For one morning when the chasm seemed to be widest, there was a long talk on bhakti—that perfect identity with the Beloved that the devotion of Râyá Râmânanda the Bengali nobleman before Chaitanya so beautifully illustrates—

"Four eyes met. There were changes in two souls.

And now I cannot remember whether he is a man

And I a woman, or he a woman and I a man!

All I know is, there were two, Love came, and there is one!"

It was that same morning that he talked of the Babists of Persia,—in their era of martyrdom—of the woman who inspired and the man who worshipped and worked. And doubtless then he expatiated on that theory of his—somewhat quaint and surprising to unaccustomed minds, not so much for the matter of the statement, as for the explicitness of the expression,

—of the greatness and goodness of the young, who can love without seeking personal expression for their love, and their high potentiality.

Another day coming at sunrise when the snows could be seen, dawn-lighted, from the garden, it was Siva and Umâ on whom he dwelt,—and that was Siva, up there, the white snow-peaks, and the light that fell upon Him was the Mother of the World! For a thought on which at this time he was dwelling much was that God *is* the Universe,—not within it, or outside it, and not the universe God or the image of God—but He it, and the All.

Sometimes all through the summer he would sit for hours telling us stories, those cradle-tales of Hinduism, whose function is not at all that of our nursery fictions, but much more, like the man-making myths of the old Hellenic world. Best of all these I thought was the story of Suka, and we looked on the Siva-mountains and the bleak scenery of Almora the evening we heard it for the first time.

Suka, the typical Paramahamsa, refused to be born for fifteen years, because he knew that his birth would mean his mother's death.* Then his father appealed to Umâ, the Divine mother. She was perpetually tearing down the veil of Mâyâ before the hidden Saint, and Vyâsa pleaded that She should cease this, or his son would never come to birth. Umâ consented, for one moment only and that moment the child was born. He came forth a young man sixteen years of age, unclothed, and went straight forward, knowing neither his father nor his mother, straight on, followed by Vyâsa. Then, coming round a mountain-pass his body melted away from him, because it was no different from the universe, and his father following and crying, "Oh my son! Oh my son!" was answered only by the echo, "Om! Om! Om!"—among the rocks. Then Suka

* The reader may question this version of the story of Suka. But the Sister Niveditâ, as far as we can judge has put the facts here thus, intentionally, either to make it appear moral natural or to suggest the great love that Suka had in his heart; for he (Suka) knew he would leave father, mother, kindred, home and all for the love of God, as soon as he was born, causing death-like pangs to them, especially to his mother's heart. The reader should remember this also while reading the last part of the story.

resumed his body, and came to his father to get knowledge from him. But Vyâsa found that he had none for him, and sent him to Janaka, king of Mithilâ, the father of Sitâ, if perchance he might have some to give. Three days he sat outside the royal gates, unheaded, without a change of expression or of look. The fourth day he was suddenly admitted to the king's presence with *éclat*. Still there was no change.

Then as a test, the powerful sage who was the kings prime minister, translated himself into a beautiful woman, so beautiful that every one present had to turn away from the sight of her, and none dared speak. But Suka went up to her and drew her to sit beside him on his mat, while he talked to her of God.

Then the minister turned to Janaka saying, "Know, oh King, if you seek the greatest man on earth, this is he!"

"There is little more told of the life of Suka. He is the ideal Paramahamsa. To him alone amongst men was it given to drink a handful of the waters of that one undivided Ocean of Sat-Chit-Ananda—existence, knowledge and bliss absolute! Most saints die, having heard only the thunder of Its waves upon the shore. A few gain the vision—and still fewer, taste of It. But he drank of the Sea of Bliss!"

Suka was indeed the Swami's saint. He was the type, to him, of that highest realisation to which life and the world are merely play. Long after, we learned how Sri Râmakrishna had spoken of him in his boyhood as, "My Suka." And never can I forget the look, as of one gazing far into depths of joy, with which he once stood and quoted the words of Siva, in praise of the deep spiritual significance of the Bhagavad-Gitâ, and of the greatness of Suka —"I know, the real meaning of the teachings of the Bhagavad-Gitâ, and Suka knows, and *perhaps* Vyâsa knows—a little!"

Another day in Almora the Swami talked of the great humanising lives that had arisen in Bengal, at the long inrolling wash of the first wave of modern conciousness on the ancient shores of Hindu culture. Of Ram Mohan Roy we had already heard from him at Nani Tal. And now of the Pundit Vidyâsâgar he exclaimed "There is not a man of my age in Northern India, on whom his shadow has not fallen!" It was a great joy to him to remember that these men and Sri Râmakrishna had all been born within a few miles of each other.

The Swami introduced Vidyâsâgar to us now as "the hero of widow remarriage, and of the abolition of polygamy." But his favourite story about him was of that day when he went home from the Legislative Council, pondering over the question of whether or not to adopt English dress on such occasions. Suddenly some one came up to a fat Mogul who was proceeding homewards in leisurely and pompous fashion, in front of him, with the news "Sir, your house is on fire!" The Mogul went neither faster nor slower for this information, and presently the messenger contrived to express a discreet astonishment. Whereupon his master turned on him angrily, "Wretch!" he said, "am I to abandon the gait of my ancestors, because a few sticks happen to be burning?" And Vidyâsâgar, walking behind, determined to stick to the chudder, dhoti and sandals, not even adopting coat and slippers.

The picture of Vidyâsâgar going into retreat for a month for the study of the Shâstras, (Scriptures), when his mother had suggested to him the re-marriage of child-widows, was very forcible. "He came out of his retirement of opinion that they were *not* against such re-marriage, and he obtained the signatures of the pundits that they agreed in this opinion. Then the action of certain native princes led the pundits to abandon their own signatures, so that, had the Government not determined to assist the movement, it could not have been carried—and now," added the Swami, " the difficulty has an economic rather than a social basis."

We could believe that a man who was able to discredit polygamy by moral force alone, was "intensely spiritual." And it was wonderful indeed to realise the Indian indifference to a formal creed, when we heard how this giant was driven by the famine of 1864,—when 140000 people died of hunger and disease,—to have nothing more to do with God, and become entirely agnostic in thought.

With this man, as one of the educators of Bengal, the Swami coupled the name of *David*

*Hare,* the old Scots-man and atheist to whom the clergy of Calcutta refused Christian burial. He had died of nursing an old pupil through cholera. So his own boys carried his dead body and buried it in a swamp, and made the grave a place of pilgrimage. That place has now become College Square, the educational centre and his school is now within the University. And to this day, Calcutta students make pilgrimage to the tomb.

On this day we took advantage of the natural turn of the conversation to cross-question the Swami as to the possible influence that Christianity might have exerted over himself. He was much amused to hear that such a statement had been hazarded, and told us with much pride of his only contact with missionary influences, in the person of his old Scotch master, Mr. Hastie. This hot-headed old man lived on nothing, and regarded his room as his boy's home as much as his own. It was he who had first sent the Swami to Sri Râmakrishna, and towards the end of his stay in India he used to say "Yes my boy, you were right, you were right !—It is true that all is God !" "I am *proud* of him!"—cried the Swami, "but I don't think you could say that he had Christianised me much!" It appeared, indeed, that he had only been his pupil for some six months, having attended college so irregularly that the Presidency College refused to send him up for his degree, though he undertook to pass!

We heard charming stories, too, on less serious subjects. There was the lodging-house in an American city for instance, where he had had to cook his own food, and where he would meet, in the course of operations, "an actress who ate roast turkey everyday, and a husband and wife who lived by making ghosts". And when the Swami remonstrated with the husband, and tried to persuade him to give up deceiving people, saying "You *ought* not to do this!" the wife would come up behind, and say eagerly "Yes Sir! that's just what I tell him; for *he* makes all the ghosts, and Mrs. Williams takes all the money!"

He told us also of a young engineer, an educated man, who, at a spiritualistic gathering, "when the fat Mrs. Williams appeared from behind the screen as his thin mother, exclaimed 'Mother dear, how you *have* grown in the spirit-world!"

"At this," said the Swami, "my heart broke, for I thought there could be no hope for the man." But never at a loss, he told the story of a Russian painter, who was ordered to paint the picture of a peasant's dead father, the only description given being, "Man! don't I tell you he had a wart on his nose?" When at last, therefore, the painter had made a portrait of some stray peasant, and affixed a large wart to the nose, the picture was declared to be ready, and the son was told to come and see it. He stood in front of it, greatly overcome, and said "Father! Father! how changed you are since I saw you last!" After this, the young engineer would never speak to the Swami again, which showed at least that he could see the point of a story. But at this, the Hindu monk was genuinely astonished.

In spite of such general interests, however, the inner strife grew high, and the thought pressed on the mind of one of the older members of our party that the Master himself needed service and peace. Many times he spoke with wonder of the torture of life, and who can say how many signs there were, of bitter need? A word or two was spoken—little, but enough—and he, after many hours, came back and told us that he longed for quiet, and would go alone to the forests and find soothing.

And then, looking up, he saw the young moon shinning above us, and he said "The Mohammedans think much of the new moon. Let us also, with the new moon, begin a new life!" And he blessed his daughter with a great blessing, so that she, thinking that her old relationship was broken, nor dreaming that a new and deeper life was being given to it, knew only that the hour was strange and passing sweet.

And so that strife was ended, and for all views and opinions of the Swami, there was room made thenceforth, that they might be held and examined, and determined on at leisure, however impossible or unpleasing they might seem at the first.

*May 25.*

He went. It was Wednesday. And on

Saturday he came back. He had been in the silence of the forests ten hours each day, but on returning to his tent in the evenings, he had been surrounded with so much eager attendance as to break the mood, and he had fled. Yes, he was radiant. He had discovered in himself the old-time sannyâsi, able to go barefoot, and endure heat, cold, and scanty fare, unspoilt by the West. This, and what else he had got, was enough for the present, and we left him, under the eucalyptus trees, and amongst the tea-roses, in Mr. Sevier's garden, full of gratitude and peace.

*May 30.*

The following Monday he went away, with his host and hostess, on a week's visit, and we were left in Almora to read, and draw, and botanise. One evening in that week, we sat talking after dinner. Our thoughts were curiously with the 'In Memoriam', and one of us read aloud—

*June, 2nd.*

"Yet in these ears, till hearing dies,
One set slow bell will seem to toll

The passing of the sweetest soul
That ever looked with human eyes.
I hear it now, and o'er and o'er,
Eternal greetings to the dead;
And 'Ave, Ave, Ave,' said,
'Adieu, Adieu,' for evermore."

It was the very hour at which, in the distant south, one soul of our own circle was passing out of this little church visible of ours, into some finer radiance and more triumphant manifestation, perhaps, in the closer presence possible beyond. But we did not know it yet. Still another day the dark shadow of, we knew not what hung over us. And then, as we sat working on Friday morning, the telegram came, a day late, that said—"Goodwin died last night at Ootacamund." Our poor friend had, it appeared, been one of the first victims of what was to prove an epidemic of typhoid fever. And it seemed that with his last breath he had spoken of the Swami, and longed for his presence by his side.

*June 5th.*

On Sunday evening, the Swami came

home. Through our gate and over the terrace his way brought him, and there we sat and talked with him a moment. He did not know our news, but a great darkness hung over him already, and presently he broke the silence to remind us of that saint who had called the cobra's bite "messenger from the Beloved," one whom he had loved, second only to Sri Râmakrishna himself. "I have just," he said, "received a letter that says: Paohâri Bâbâ has completed all his sacrifices with the sacrifice of his own body. He has burnt himself in his sacrificial fire." "Swami!" exclaimed someone from amongst his listeners, "wasn't that very wrong?"

"How can I tell?" said the Swami, speaking in great agitation. "He was too great a man for me to judge. He knew himself what he was doing."

Very little was said after this, and the party of monks passed on. Not yet had the other news been broken.

*June 6th.*

Next morning he came early, in a great

mood. He had been up, he said afterwards, since four. And one went out to meet him, and told him, of Mr. Goodwin's death. The blow fell quietly. Some days later, he refused to stay in the place where he had received it, and complained of the weakness that brought the image of his most faithful disciple constantly into his mind. It was no more manly, he protested, to be thus ridden by one's memory, than to retain the characteristics of the fish or the dog. Man must conquer this illusion, and know that the dead are here beside us and with us, as much as ever. It is their absence and separation that are a myth. And then he would break out again with some bitter utterance against the folly of imagining Personal Will to guide the universe. "As if," he exclaimed, "it would not be one's right and duty to fight such a God and slay Him, for killing Goodwin !—And Goodwin, if he had lived, could have done so much !" And in India one was free to recognise this as the most religious, because the most unflinchingly truthful mood of all !

And while I speak of this utterance, I may perhaps put beside it another, that I heard a year later, spoken out of the same fierce wonder at the dreams with which we comfort ourselves. "Why!" he said, then, "Every petty magistrate and officer is allowed his period of retirement and rest. Only God, The Eternal Magistrate, must sit judging for ever, and never go free!"

But in these first hours, the Swami was calm about his loss, and sat down and chatted quietly with us. He was full that morning of *bhakti* passing into asceticism, the divine passion that carries the soul on its high tides, far out of reach of persons, yet leaves it again, struggling to avoid those sweet snares of personality.

What he said that morning of renunciation proved a hard gospel to one of those who listened, and when he came again she put it to him as her conviction that to love without attachment involved no pain, and was in itself ideal.

He turned on her with a sudden solemnity. "What is this idea of *bhakti* without renunciation?" he said. "It is most pernicious!" and standing there for an hour or more, he talked of the awful self-discipline that one must impose on oneself, if one would indeed be unattached, of the requisite nakedness of selfish motives, and of the danger that at any moment the most flower-like soul might have its petals soiled with the grosser stains of life. He told the story of an Indian nun who was asked when a man could be certain of safety on this road, and who sent back, for answer, a little plate of ashes. For the fight against passion was long and fierce, and at any moment the conqueror might become the conquered.

And as he talked, it seemed that this banner of renunciation was the flag of a great victory, that poverty and self-mastery were the only fit raiment for the soul that would wed the Eternal Bridegroom, and that life was a long opportunity for giving, and the thing not taken away from us was to be mourned as lost. Weeks afterwards, in Kashmir, when he was again talking in some kindred fashion, one of us ventured to ask him if the feeling he thus roused were not that worship of pain that Europe abhors as morbid.

"Is the worship of pleasure, then, so noble?" was his immediate answer. "But indeed," he added, after a pause, "we worship neither pain nor pleasure. We seek through either to come at that which transcends them both."

*June 9th.*

This Thursday morning there was a talk on Krishna. It was characteristic of the Swami's mind, and characteristic also of the Hindu culture from which he had sprung, that he could lend himself to the enjoyment and portrayal of an idea one day, that the next would see submitted to a pitiless analysis and left slain upon the field. He was a sharer to the full in the belief of his people that, provided an idea was spiritually true and consistent, it mattered very little about its objective actuality. And this mode of thought had first been suggested to him, in his boyhood, by his own Master. He had mentioned some doubt as to the authenticity of a certain religious history. "What!" said Sri Râmakrishna, "do you not then think that those who could conceive such ideas must have been the thing itself?"

The existence of Krishna, then, like that of Christ, he often told us 'in the general way' he doubted. Buddha and Mahommed alone, amongst religious teachers, had been fortunate enough to have 'enemies as well as friends', so that their historical careers were beyond dispute. As for Krishna, he was the most shadowy of all. A poet, a cowherd, a great ruler, a warrior, and a sage had all perhaps been merged in one beautiful figure, holding the Gitâ in his hand.

But to-day, Krishna was "the most perfect of the avatars." And a wonderful picture followed, of the charioteer who reined in his horses, while he surveyed the field of battle and in one brief glance noted the disposition of the forces, at the same moment that he commenced to utter to his royal pupil the deep spiritual truths of the Gitâ.

And indeed as we went through the country-sides of northern India this summer, we had many chances of noting how deep this Krishna-myth had set its mark upon the people. The songs that dancers chanted as they danced, in the roadside hamlets, were all of Râdhâ and Krishna. And the Swami was fond of a statement, as to which we, of course, could have no opinion, that the Krishna-worshippers of India had exhausted the possibilities of the romantic motive in lyric poetry.

Is that curious old story of the Gopis, then, really a fragment of some pastoral worship, absorbed by a more modern system, and persistently living on, in all its dramatic tenderness and mirth, into the glare of the nineteenth century?

But throughout these days, the Swami was fretting to be away and alone. The place where he had heard of Mr. Goodwin's loss was intolerable to him, and letters to be written and received constantly renewed the wound. He said one day that Sri Râmakrishna, while seeming to be all *bhakti* was really, within, all *jnâna;* but he himself, apparently all *jnâna,* was full of *bhakti,* and that thereby he was apt to be as weak as any woman.

One day he carried off a few faulty lines of some one's writing, and brought back a little poem, which was sent to the widowed mother, as his memorial of her son.

Requiescat in Pace!
Speed forth, O soul! upon thy
star-strewn path,
Speed, blissful one, where thought
is ever free,
Where time and sense no longer
mist the view,
Eternal peace and blessings be on thee!
Thy service true, complete thy sacrifice,
Thy home the heart of love
transcendent find,
Remembrance sweet, that tells all
space and time,
Like alter-roses, fill thy place behind.
Thy bonds are broke, thy quest in bliss
is found.
And—one with that which comes as
Death and Life,—
Thou helpful one! unselfish e'er on earth,
Ahead, still aid with love this world
of strife.

And then, because there was nothing left of the original, and he feared that she who was corrected (because *her* lines had been "in three metres") might be hurt, he expatiated, long and earnestly upon the theme that it was so much greater to feel poetically than merely to string syllables together in rhyme and metre! He might be very severe on a sympathy or an opinion that seemed in his eyes sentimental or false. But an effort that failed found always in the Master its warmest advocate and tenderest defence.

And how happy was that acknowledgment of the bereaved mother to him, when, in the midst of her sorrow she wrote and thanked him for the character of his influence over the son who had died so far away!

*June, 10th.*

It was our last afternoon at Almora that we heard the story of the fatal illness of Sri Râmakrishna. Dr. Mohendra Lall Sirkar had been called in, and had pronounced the disease to be cancer of the throat, leaving the young disciples with many warnings as to its infectious nature. Half an hour later, "Noren", as he then was, came in and found them huddled together, discussing the dangers of the case. He listened to what they had been told, and then, looking down, saw at his feet the cup of gruel that had been partly taken by Sri Râmakrishna and which must have contained in it, the germs of the fatal discharges of mucous and *pus*, as it came out in his baffled attempts to swallow the thing, on account of the stricture of the food-passage in the throat. He picked it up, and drank from it, before them all. Never was the infection of cancer mentioned amongst the disciples again.

---

# CHAPTER IV.

## ON THE WAY TO KATHGODAM.

*June 11th.*

On Saturday morning we left Almora. It took us two days and a half to reach Kathgodam. How beautiful the journey was! Dim, almost tropical, forests, troops of monkeys, and the ever-wondrous Indian night.

Somewhere *en route* near a curious old water-mill and deserted forge, the Swami told *Dhirâ Mâtâ* of a legend that spoke of this hill-side as haunted by a race of centaur-like phantoms, and of an experience known to him, by which one had first seen forms there, and only afterwards heard the folk-tale.

The roses were gone by this time, but a flower was in bloom that crumbled at a touch, and he pointed this out, because of its wealth of associations in Indian poetry.

*June 12th.*

On Sunday afternoon we rested, near the

Plains, in what we took to be an out-of-the-way hotel, above a lake and fall, and there he translated for us the Rudra-prayer.

"From the Unreal lead us to the Real.
From darkness lead us unto light.
From death lead us to immortality.
Reach us through and through our self.
And evermore protect us—Oh Thou
Terrible !—
From ignorance, by Thy sweet
compassionate Face."

He hesitated a long time over the fourth line, thinking of rendering it, "Embrace us in the heart of our heart". But at last he put his perplexity to us, saying shyly, "The real meaning is Reach us through and through our-self." He had evidently feared that this sentence, with its extraordinary intensity, might not make good sense in English. But our un-hesitating choice of that afternoon has received a deep confirmation in my own eyes, since I have understood that a more literal rendering would be, "O Thou who art manifest only unto Thyself, manifest Thyself also unto us!" I now regard his translation as a rapid and direct transcript of the experience of *Samadhi* itself. It tears the living heart out of the Sanskrit, as it were, and renders it again in an English form.

It was indeed an afternoon of translations, and he gave us fragments of the great benediction after mourning, which is one of the most beautiful of the Hindu sacraments;

"The blissful winds are sweet to us.
The seas are showering bliss on us.
May the corn in our fields bring bliss to us.
May the plants and herbs bring bliss to us.
May the cattle give us bliss.
O Father in Heaven be Thou blissful unto us!
The very dust of the earth is full of bliss.
(And then, the voice dying down into meditation),—
It is all bliss—all bliss—all bliss."

And again we had Soor Das' Song which the Swami heard from the Nautch-girl at Khetri:

O Lord, look not upon my evil qualities!
Thy name, O Lord, is Same-sightedness.
Make of us both the same Brahman!
One drop of water is in the sacred Jumna,

And another is foul in the ditch by the roadside,
But, when they fall into the Ganges, both alike become holy.
So Lord, look not upon my evil qualities,
Thy name, O Lord, is Same-sightedness,
Make of us both the same Brahman!
One piece of iron is the image in the temple,
And another is the knife in the hand of the butcher,
But when they touch the philosopher's stone, both alike turn to gold.
So Lord, look not upon my evil qualities,
Thy name, O Lord, is Samesightedness.
Make of us both the same Brahman!

Was it that same day, or some other, that he told us of the old Sannyâsin in Benares, who saw him annoyed by troops of monkeys, and, afraid that he might turn and run, shouted, "Always face the brute!"?

Those journeys were delightful. We were always sorry to reach a destination. At this time, it took us a whole afternoon to cross the Terai by rail,—that strip of malarial country, on which, as he reminded us, Buddha had been born. As we had come down the mountain-roads, we had met parties of country-folk, fleeing to the upper hills, with their families and all their goods, to escape the fever which would be upon them with the rains. And now, in the train, there was the gradual change of vegetation to watch, and the Master's pleasure, greater than that of any proprietor, in showing us the wild peacocks, or here and there an elephant, or a train of camels.

Quickly enough, we came back to the palm-zone. Already we had reached the yuccas and cactus the day before, and deodar-cedars we should not see again, till distant Acchabal.

---

# CHAPTER V

## ON THE WAY TO BARAMULLA

*Persons* :—The Swami Vivekananda ; Guru-bhâis, and disciples.
A party of Europeans, amongst whom were Dhirâ Mâtâ, the 'Steady Mother'; 'One whose name was Jayâ'; and Niveditâ.
*Place* :—From Bareilly to Baramulla, Kashmir.
*Time* :—June 14th to 20th, 1898.

*June 14th.*

We entered the Punjab next day, and great was the Swami's excitement at the fact. It almost seemed as if he had been born there, so close and special was his love for this province. He talked of the girls at their spinning wheels, listening to the "Sohum ! Sohum !—I am He ! I am He !" Then, by a swift transition he turned to the far past, and unrolled for us the great historic panorama of the advance of the Greeks on the Indus, the rise of Chandragupta, and the development of the Buddhistic empire. He was determined this summer to find his way to Attock, and see with his own eyes the spot at which Alexander was turned back. He described to us the Gandhara sculptures, which he must have seen in the Lahore Museum the year before, and lost himself in indignant repudiation of the absurd European claim that India had ever sat at the feet of Greece in things artistic.

Then there were flying glimpses of long expected cities,—Ludhiana, where certain trusty English disciples had lived as children; Lahore, where his Indian lectures had ended; and so on. We came, too, upon the dry gravel beds of many rivers and learnt that the space between one pair was called the Doab and the area containing them all, the Punjaub. It was at twilight, crossing one of these stony tracts, that he told us of that great vision which came to him years ago, while he was still new to the ways of the life of a monk, giving back to him, as he always afterwards believed, the ancient mode of Sanskrit chanting.

"It was evening," he said, "in that age when the Aryans had only reached the Indus.

I saw an old man seated on the bank of the great river. Wave upon wave of darkness was rolling in upon him, and he was chanting from the Rik Veda. Then I awoke, and went on chanting. They were the tones that we used long ago."

Many months later, one of those who listened, heard the story of this vision once more from the Swami; and it seemed to her then, with her gathered insight into his method of thought, that it had been an experience of immense subjective importance. Perhaps it was a token to him of a transcendent continuity in the spiritual experience, forbidding it to be baffled even by the lapse of millenniums and the breaking of many life-threads. If so, one could not expect him to be explicit on the point. Those who were constantly preoccupied with imagination regarding their own past, always aroused his contempt. But on this second occasion of telling the story, he gave a glimpse of it, from a very different point of view.

"Sankarâcharya," he was saying, "had caught the rhythm of the Vedas, the national cadence. Indeed I always imagine", he went on suddenly, with dreamy voice and far away look, "I always imagine that he had some vision such as mine when he was young, and recovered the ancient music that way. Anyway, his whole life's work is nothing but that, the throbbing of the beauty of the Vedas and Upanishads."

Speeches like this were of course purely speculative, and he himself could never bear to be reminded of the theories to which he thus in moments of emotion and impulse, gave chance birth. To others however they would often seem not valueless.

"Vivekananda is nothing" exclaimed one of his admirers in the distant West, "if not a breaker of bondage!"—and a trifling incident of this day's journey recalls the words. At a station entering the Punjab, he called to him a Mahommedan vendor of food, and bought from his hand, and ate.

From Rawalpindi to Murree, we went by tonga, and there we spent some days before setting out for Kashmir. Here the Swami came to the conclusion that any effort which he might make to induce the orthodox to accept a

European as a fellow-disciple, or in the direction of woman's education, had better be made in Bengal. The distrust of the foreigner was too strong in Panjab, to admit of work succeeding there. He was much occupied by this question, from time to time, and would sometimes remark on the paradox presented by the Bengali combination of political antagonism to the English, and readiness to love and trust.

We had reached Murree on Wednesday afternoon, June the 15th. It was again Saturday, June the 18th, when we set out for Kashmir.

*June 18th.*

One of our party was ill, and that first day we went but a short distance, and stopped at Dulai, the first dark bungalow across the border. It was a curious moment, leaving British India behind, with the crossing of a dusty, sunbaked bridge. We were soon to have a vivid realisation of just how much and just how little this demarcation meant.

We were now in the valley of the Jhelum. Our whole journey, from Kohala to Baramulla, was to run through a narrow, twisting, mountain-pass, the rapidly-rising ravine of this river. Here, at Dulai, the speed of the current was terrific, and huge water-smoothed pebbles formed a great shingle.

Most of the afternoon, we were compelled by a storm to spend indoors, and a new chapter was opened at Dulai, in our knowledge of Hinduism, for the Swami told us, gravely and frankly, of its modern abuses, and spoke of his own uncompromising hostility to those evil practices which pass under the name of *Vâmâ-châra*.

When we asked how Sri Râmakrishna,—who never could bear to condemn the hope of any man,—had looked at these things, he told us that 'the old man' had said "Well, well! but every house may have a scavengers' entrance!" And he pointed out that all sects of *diabolism,* in any country, belonged to this class. It was a terrible but necessary revelation, that never required to be repeated, and it has been related here, in its true place, in order that none may be able to say that he deceived those who trusted him, as to the worst things that might be urged against any of his people or their creeds.

*June 19th.*

We took it in turns to drive with the Swami in his tonga, and this next day seemed full of reminiscence.

He talked of *Brahmavidyâ*, the vision of the One, the Alone-Real, and told how love was the only cure for evil. He had had a schoolfellow, who grew up and became rich, but lost his health. It was an obscure disease, sapping his energy and vitality daily, yet altogether baffling the skill of the doctors. At last, because he knew that the Swami had always been religious, and men turn to religion when all else fails, he sent to beg him to come to him. When the Master reached him, a curious thing happened. There came to his mind a text—"Him the Brahmin conquers, who thinks that he is separate from the Brahmin. Him the Kshatriya conquers, who thinks that he is separate from the Kshatriya. And him the Universe conquers who thinks that he is separate from the Universe." And the sick man grasped this, and recovered. "And so," said the Swami, "though I often say strange things and angry things, yet remember that in my heart I never seriously mean to preach anything but love! All these things will come right, only when we realise that we love each other."

Was it then, or the day before, that, talking of the Great God, he told us how when he was a child, his mother would sigh over his naughtiness, and say "so many prayers and austerities, and instead of a good soul, Siva has sent me you!" till he was hypnotised into a belief that he was really one of Siva's demons. He thought that for a punishment, he had been banished for awhile from Siva's heaven, and that his one effort in life must be to go back there. His first act of sacrilege, he told us once, had been committed at the age of five, when we embarked on a stormy argument with his mother, to the effect that when his right hand was soiled with eating, it would be cleaner to lift his tumbler of water with the left. For this or similar perversities, her most drastic remedy was to put him under the watertap, and while cold water was pouring over his head, to say "Siva! Siva!" This, he said, never failed of its effect. The prayer would remind him of his exile, and he would say to himself "No, no, not this time again!" and so return to quiet and obedience.

He had a surpassing love for Mahâdeva, and once he said of the Indian women of the future that if, amidst their new tasks they would only remember now and then to say "Siva! Siva!" it would be worship enough. The very air of the Himalayas was charged, for him, with the image of that "eternal meditation" that no thought of pleasure could break. And he understood, he said, for the first time this summer, the meaning of the nature-story that made the Ganges fall on the head of the Great God, and wander in and out amongst His matted locks, before she found an outlet on the plains below. He had searched long, he said, for the words that the rivers and waterfalls uttered, amongst the mountains, before he had realised that it was the eternal cry "Bom! Bom! Hara! Hara!" "Yes!" he said of Siva one day, "He is the Great God, calm, beautiful, and silent! and I am His great worshipper."

Again his subject was marriage, as the type of the soul's relation to God.—"This is why," he exclaimed, "though the love of a mother is in some ways greater, yet the whole world takes the love of man and woman as the type. *No other has such tremendous idealising power.* The beloved actually becomes what he is imagined to be. This love transforms its object."

Then the talk strayed to national types, and he spoke of the joy with which the returning traveller greets once more the sight of the men and women of his own country. The whole of life has been a sub-conscious education to enable one to understand in these every faintest ripple of expression in face and form.

And again we passed a group of sannyâsins going on foot, and he broke out into fierce invective against asceticism as "savagery." It is a peculiarity of India that only the religious life is perfectly conscious and fully developed. In other lands, a man will undergo as many hardships, in order to win success in business, or enterprise, or even in sport, as these men were probably enduring. But the sight of wayfares doing slow miles on foot in the name of their ideals, seemed to rouse in his mind a train of painful associations, and he grew impatient on behalf of humanity, at "the torture of religion." Then again the mood passed, as suddenly as it had arisen, and gave place to the equally strong statement of the conviction that were it not for this "savagery," luxury would have robbed man of all his manliness.

We stopped that evening at Uri dâk-bungalow, and in the twilight, we all walked in the meadows and the bazar. How beautiful the place was ! A little mud fortress—exactly of the European feudal pattern—overhung the footway as it swept into a great open theatre of field and hill. Along the road, above the river, lay the bazar, and we returned to the bungalow by a path across the fields, past cottages in whose gardens the roses were in bloom. As we came, too, it would happen that there and there, some child, more venturesome than other, would play with us.

*June 20.*

The next day, driving through the most beautiful part of the Pass, and seeing cathedral rocks and an old ruined temple of the Sun, we reached Baramulla. The legend is that the Vale of Kashmir was once a lake, and that at this point the Divine Boar pierced the mountains with his tusks, and let the Jhelum go free. Another piece of geography in the form of myth. Or is it also prehistoric history?

---

# CHAPTER VI.

## THE VALE OF KASHMIR.

Persons :—The Swami Vivekananda and a party of Europeans, amongst whom were Dhirâ Mâtâ—the 'Steady Mother,' 'One whose name was Jayâ,' and Niveditâ.
*Time* :—June 20th to June 22nd.
*Place* :—The River Jhelum—Baramulla to Srinagar.

"It is said that the Lord Himself is the weight on the side of the fortunate !" cried the Swami in high glee, returning to our room at the dâkbungalow, and sitting down, with his umbrella on his knees. As he had brought no companion, he had himself to perform all the ordinary little masculine offices, and he had gone out of hire *dungas,* and do what was necessary. But he had immediately fallen in with a man, who, on hearing his name, had undertaken the whole business, and sent him back, free of responsibility.

So we enjoyed the day. We drank

Kashmiri tea out of a *Sâmâvar* and ate the jam of the country, and at about four o'clock we entered into possession of a flotilla of *dungas,* three in number, on which presently we set forth for Srinagar. The first evening, however we were moored by the garden of the Swami's friend, and there we're played with the children, and gathered forget-me-nots, and watched a circle of peasants, singing, at some harvest-game in the freshly-cut cornfields. The Swami, returning to his boat about eleven, could still as he passed us in the dark, hear the end of our warm discussion about the effect of the introduction of money on rural peoples.

We found ourselves, next day, in the midst of a beautiful valley, ringed round with snow-mountains. This is known as the Vale of Kashmir, but it might be more accurately described, perhaps, as the Vale of Srinagar. The city of Islamabad had its own valley, higher up the river, and to reach it we had to wind in and out amongst the mountains. The sky above was of the bluest of the blue, and the water-road along which we travelled, was also, perforce, blue. Sometimes our way lay through great green tangles of lotus-leaves, with a rosy flower or two, and on each side stretched the fields, in some of which, as we came, they were reaping. The whole was a symphony in blue and green and white, so exquisitely pure and vivid that for a while the response of the soul to its beauty was almost pain!

That first morning, taking a long walk across the fields, we came upon an immense chennaar tree, standing in the midst of a wide pasture. It really looked as if the passage through it might shelter the proverbial twenty cows! The Swami fell to architectural visions of how it might be fitted up as a dwelling-place for a hermit. A small cottage might in fact have been built in the hollow of this living tree. And then he talked of meditation, in a way to consecrate every chennaar we should ever see.

We turned, with him, into the neighbouring farm-yard. There we found, seated under a tree, a singularly handsome elderly woman. She wore the crimson coronet and white veil of the Kashmiri wife, and sat spinning wool, while round her, helping here, were her two daughters-in-law and their children. The Swami had called at this farm once before, in the previous autumn, and often spoken, since, of the faith and pride of this very woman. He had begged for water, which she had at once given him. Then, before going, he had asked her quickly, "And what, Mother, is your religion?" "I thank God, Sir!" had rung out the old voice, in pride and triumph, "by the mercy of the Lord, I am a Mussalmân!" The whole family received him now, as an old friend, and were ready to show every courtesy to the friends he had brought. The journey to Srinagar took two to three days, and one evening, as we walked in the fields before supper, one who had seen the Kâlighât, complained to the Master of the abandonment of feeling there, which had jarred on her. "*Why* do they kiss the ground before the Images?" she exclaimed. The Swami had been pointing to the crop of *til*,—which he thought to have been the original of the English dill,—and calling it "the oldest oil-bearing seed of the Aryans." But at this question, he dropped the little blue flower from his hands, and a great hush came over his voice, as he stood still and said. "Is it not the same thing to kiss the ground before that Image, as to kiss the ground before these mountains?"

Our Master had promised that before the end of the summer he would take us into retreat, and teach us to meditate. We had now to go Srinagar for a long-accumulating mail, and the question rose as to the arrangement of the holiday. It was decided that we should first see the country, and afterwards make the retreat.

The first evening in Srinagar we dined out, with some Bengali officials and in course of conversation, one of the western guests, maintained that the history of every nation illustrated and evolved certain ideals, to which the people of that nation should hold themselves true. It was very curious to see how the Hindus present objected to this. To them it was clearly a bondage, to which the mind of man could not permanently submit itself. Indeed, in their revolt against the fetters of the doctrine, they appeared to be unable to do justice to the idea itself. At last the Swami intervened. "I think you must admit," he said, "that the ultimate unit is psychological. This is much more permanent than the geographical." And then he spoke of cases known to us all, of one of whom he always though as the most typical "Christian" he had ever seen, yet she was a Bengali woman, and of another, born in the West, who was 'a better Hindu than himself.' And was not this, after all, the ideal state of things, that each should be born in the other's country to spread the given ideal as far as it could be carried?

---

# CHAPTER VII.

## LIFE AT SRINAGAR.

*Place* :—Srinagar.
*Time* :—June 22nd to July 15th, 1898.

In the mornings, we still had long talks, as before—sometimes it would be the different religious periods through which Kashmir had passed, or the morality of Buddhism, or the history of Siva-worship, or perhaps the position of Srinagar under Kanishka.

Once he was talking with one of us about Buddhism, and he suddenly said "the fact is Buddhism tried to do, in the time of Asoka, what the world never was ready for till now!" He referred to the federalisation of religions. It was a wonderful picture, this, of the religious imperialism of Asoka, broken down, time and again, by successive waves of Christianity and Mahammedanism, each claiming exclusive rights over the conscience of mankind, and finally to seem to have a possibility, within measurable distance of time, to-day!

Another time, the talk was of Genghis or Chenghiz Khan, the conqueror from Central Asia. "You hear people talk of him as a vulgar aggressor," he cried passionately, "but that is not true! They are never greedy or vulgar, these great souls! He was inspired with the thought of unity, and he wanted to unify his world. Yes, Napoleon was cast in the same mould. And another, Alexander. Only those three, or perhaps one soul, manifesting itself in three different conquests!" And then he passed on to speak of that one soul whom he believed to have come again and again in religion, charged with the divine impulse to bring about the unity of man in God.

At this time, the transfer of the Prabuddha Bhârata, from Madras to the newly established *Ashrama* at Mâyâvati was much in all our thoughts. The Swami had always had a special love for this paper, as the beautiful name he had given it indicated. He had always been eager, too, for the establishment of organs of his own. The value of the journal in the education of Modern India, was perfectly evident to him, and he felt that his Master's message and mode of thought required to be spread by this means, as well as by preaching and by work. Day after day, therefore he would dream about the future of his papers, as about the work of its various centres. Day after day he would talk of the forthcoming first number, under the new editorship of Swami Svarupânanda. And one afternoon he brought to us, as we sat together, a paper on which, he said, he had "tried to write a letter, but it would come this way!"—

To the Awakened India.

Once more awake!

For sleep it was,—not death,—to bring thee life anew, and rest to lotus-eyes, for visions daring yet. The world, in need, awaits, Oh Truth, no death for thee!

Resume thy march,

With gentle feet that would not break the peaceful pose, even of the road-side dust that lies so low—yet strong, and steady, blissful, bold, and free. Awakener, ever forward! Speak thy rousing words!

Thy home is gone,
Where loving hearts had brought thee up, and watched thy growth. But fate is strong, and this the law,—All things go back to the source they sprang, their strength to renew.

Then start afresh
From the land of thy birth, where great cloud-belted snows do bless and put their strength in thee, for working wonders new. The heavenly river tune thy voice to her own eternal song; deodar shades give thee ne'er-dying peace,

And all above,
Himalaya's daughter Umâ, gentle, pure, the Mother who resides in all as power and life,—who works all works, and makes of One the world! whose mercy opens the gate to Truth, and shows the One in all,—give thee unending strength which is Infinite Love.

They bless thee, all
The seers great, whom age nor clime can claim their own, the fathers of the race,

who felt the heart of truth the same, and bravely taught to man, ill-voiced or well. Their servant, thou hast caught their secret, —'tis but One.

Then speak, Oh Love!

Before thy gentle voice so sweet, behold how visions melt, and fold on fold of dreams departs to void,—till Truth, bare Truth, in all its glory shines.

And tell the world—Awake! Arise! and dream no more!

This is the land of dreams, where *karma* weaves unthreaded garlands with our thoughts, of flowers sweet or noxious,—and none has root or stem, being born in nothing, which the softest breath of Truth drives back to primal nothingness. Be bold and face the Truth. Be one with it! Let vision cease,—or, if you cannot dream but truer dreams, which are Eternal Love and Service Free.

*June 26th.*

The Master was longing to leave us all, and go away into some place of quiet, alone.

But we not knowing this, insisted on accompanying him to the Coloured Springs, called "Kshir Bhâvani," or Milk of Mother. It was said to be the first time that Christian or Mohammedan had ever landed there, and we can never be thankful enough for the glimpse we had of it, since afterwards it was to become the most sacred of all names to us. An amusing incident was that our Mussalmân boat-men would not allow us to land with shoes on; so thoroughly Hinduistic is the Mahammedanism of Kashmir, with its forty *rishis*, and pilgrimages made fasting, to their shrines.

*June 29th.*

Another day we went off quietly by ourselves, and visited the Takt-i-Suleimân, a little temple very massively built, on the summit of a small mountain two or three thousand feet high. It was peaceful and beautiful, and the famous Floating Gardens could be seen below us, for miles around. The Takt-i-Suleimân was one of the great illustrations of the Swami's argument, when he would take up the subject of the Hindu love of nature as shown in the choice of sites for temples and architectural monuments. As he had declared, in London, that the saints lived on the hill-tops, in order to enjoy the scenery, so now he pointed out,—citing one example after another,—that our Indian people always consecrated places of peculiar beauty and importance, by making there their altars of worship. And there was no denying that the little Takt, crowning the hill that dominated the whole valley, was a case in point.

Many lovely fragments of those days come into mind, as—

"Therefore, Tulsi, take thou care to live with all, for who can tell where, or in what garb, the Lord Himself may next come to thee?"

"One God is hidden in all these, the Torturer of all, the Awakener of all, the Reservoir of all being, the One Who is bereft of all qualities."

"There the sun does not shine, nor the moon, nor the stars."

There was the story of how Râvana was advised to take the form of Râma, in order to cheat Sitâ. He answered, "Have I not thought of it? But in order to take a man's form you must meditate on him; and Râma is the Lord Himself; so, when I meditate on him, even the position of Brahmâ becomes a mere straw. How then, could I think of a woman?"

"And so", commented the Swami, "even in the commonest or most criminal life, there are these glimpses." It was ever thus. He was constantly interpreting human life as the expression of God, never insisting on the heinousness or wickedness of an act or a character.

"In that which is dark night to the rest of the world, there the man of self-control is awake. That which is life to the rest of the world is sleep to him."

Speaking of Thomas á Kempis one day, and of how he himself used to wander as a sannyâsin, with the Gitâ and the *Imitation* as his whole library, one word, he said, came back to him, inseparably associated with the name of the western monk.

"Silence! ye teachers of the world, and silence! ye prophets! Speak thou alone, O Lord, unto my soul!"

Again—

"The soft *shirisha* flower can bear the
weight of humming bees, but not of
birds—

So Umâ, don't you go and make *tapasyâ* !
come, Umâ, come ! delight and idol
of my soul !

Be seated, Mother on the lotus of my heart,

And let me take a long long look at you.

From my birth up, I am gazing,
Mother, at your face—

Know you suffering what trouble,
and pain?

Be seated, therefore, Blessed One
on the lotus of my heart,

And dwell there for evermore."

Every now and then there would be long talks about the Gitâ, "that wonderful poem, without one note in it, of weakness or unmanliness." He said one day that it was absurd to complain that knowledge was not given to women or to sudras. For the whole gist of the Upanishads was contained in the Gitâ. Without it, indeed, they could hardly be understood; and women and all castes could read the Mahâbhârata.

*July 4.*

With great fun and secrecy the Swami and his one non-American disciple prepared to celebrate The Fourth of July. A regret had been expressed in his hearing, that we had no American Flag, with which to welcome the other member of the party to breakfast, on their National Festival; and late on the afternoon of the third, he brought a *pundit durzey* in great excitement, explaining that this man would be glad to imitate it, if he were told how. The stars and stripes were very crudely represented, I fear, on the piece of cotton that was nailed, with branches of evergreens to the head of the dining-room-boat, when the Americans stepped on board for early tea, on Independence Day! But the Swami had postponed a journey, in order to be present at the little festival, and he himself contributed a poem to the addresses that were now read aloud, by way of greeting.

## To the Fourth of July.

Behold, the dark clouds melt away,
That gathered thick at night, and hung
So like a gloomy pall, above the earth!
Before thy magic touch, the world
Awakes. The birds in chorus sing.
The flowers raise their star-like crowns,
Dew-set and wave thee welcome fair.
The lakes are opening wide in love,
Their hundred-thousand lotus-eyes,
To welcome thee, with all their depth.
All hail to thee, Thou Lord of Light!
A welcome new to thee, to-day,
Oh Sun! To-day thou sheddest *Liberty!*
Bethink thee how the world did wait,
And search for thee, through time and clime—*
Some gave up home and love of friends,
And went in quest of thee, self-banished,
Through dreary oceans, through primeval forest,

---

* Clime = Climate.

Each step a struggle for life or death!
Then came the day when work bore fruit,
And worship, love and sacrifice,
Fulfilled, accepted, and complete.
And then thou, propitious, rose to shed
The light of *Freedom* on mankind!
Move on, Oh Lord, in thy resistless path!
Till thy high noon o'erspreads the world;
Till every land reflects thy light;
Till men and women, with uplifted head,
Behold their shackles broken, and
Know in springing joy, their life renewed!

*July 5.*

That evening someone pained him by counting the cherry-stones left on her plate, to see when she would be married. He, somehow, took the play in earnest, and came, the following morning, surcharged with passion for the ideal renunciation.

*July 6.*

"These shadows of home and marriage cross even *my* mind now and then!" he cried, with that tender desire to make himself one with the sinner that he so often showed. But it was across oceans of scorn for those who would glorify the householder, that he sought, on this occasion, to preach the religious life. "Is it so easy," he exclaimed, "to be Janaka? To sit on a throne absolutely unattached? Caring nothing for wealth or fame, for wife or child? One after another in the west has told me that he had reached this. But I could only say—'such great men are not born in India!'"

And then he turned to the other side.

"Never forget," he said to one of his hearers, "to say to yourself, and to teach to your children, as the difference between a firefly and the blazing sun, between the infinite ocean and a little pond, between a mustard-seed and the mountain of Meru, such is the difference between the householder and the Sannyâsin!"

"Everything is fraught with fear: Renunciation alone is fearless."

"Blessed be even the fraudulent *sâdhus*, and those who have failed to carry out their vows, in as much as they also have witnessed to the ideal, and so are in some degree the cause of the success of others!"

"Let us never, never, forget our ideal!"

At such moments, he would identify himself entirely with the thought he sought to demonstrate, and in the same sense in which a law of nature might be deemed cruel or arrogant, his exposition might have those qualities. Sitting and listening, we felt ourselves brought face to face with the invisible and absolute.

All this was on our return to Srinagar, from the real Fourth of July Celebration, which had been a visit to the Dahl Lake. There we had seen the Shâlimâr Bâgh of Nur Mahal, and the Nishât Bâgh, or Garden of Gladness, and had spent the hour of sunset quietly, amongst the green of the irises, at the foot of giant chennaar trees.

That same day, *Dhirâ Mâtâ* and she whose name was *Jayâ,* left for Gulmarg, on some personal business, and the Swami went with them, part of the way.

At nine o'clock on the evening of the following Sunday, July the 10th, the first two came back unexpectedly, and presently, from many different sources, we gathered the news that the Master had gone to Amarnâth by the Sonamarg route, and would return another way. He had started out penniless, but that could give no concern to his friends, in a Hindu Native state.

A disagreeable incident occurred, a day or two later, when a young man, eager to become a disciple, turned up, and insisted on being sent on to him. It was felt that this was an unwarrantable intrusion on that privacy which he had gone to seek, but as the request was persistent, it was granted, and life flowed in accustomed channels for a day or two.

*July 15.*

What were we setting out for? We were just moving to go down the river, on Friday and it was close on five in the afternoon, when the servants recognised some of their friends in the distance, and word was brought that the Swami's boat was coming towards us.

An hour later, he was with us, saying how pleasant it was to be back. The summer had been unusually hot and certain glaciers had given way, rendering the Sonamarg Route to Amarnâth impracticable. This fact had caused his return.

But from this moment dated the first of three great increments of joy and realisation that we saw in him, during our months in Kashmir. It was almost as if we could verify for ourselves the truth of that saying of his Guru—

"There is indeed a certain ignorance. It has been placed there by my Holy Mother that her work may be done. But it is only like a film of tissue paper. It might be rent at any moment."

# CHAPTER VIII.

## THE TEMPLE OF PANDRENTHAN.

*Persons* :—The Swami Vivekananda and a party of Europeans, amongst whom were Dhirâ Mâtâ, the 'Steady Mother'; One whose name was Jayâ and Niveditâ.

*Time* :—July 16th to 19th.

*Place* :—Kashmir.

*July 16.*

It fell to the lot of one of the Swami's disciples, next day, to go down the river with him in a small boat. As it went, he chanted one song after another of Râm Prasâd, and now and again, he would translate a verse.

"I call upon thee Mother.
For though his mother strike him,
The child cries "Mother! Oh Mother."

* * * *

"Though I cannot see Thee,
I am not a lost child!
I still cry 'Mother! Mother!' "—

* * * *

and then with the haughty dignity of an offended child, something that ended—"I am not the son to call *any* other woman 'Mother' !"

*July 17th.*

It must have been next day, that he came into *Dhirâ Mâtâ's dunga,* and talked of Bhakti. First it was that curious Hindu thought of Siva and Umâ in one. It is easy to give the words, but without the voice, how comparatively dead they seem ! And then there were the wonderful surroundings—picturesque Srinagar, tall Lombardy poplars, and distant snows. There, in that river-valley, some space from the foot of the great mountains, he chanted to us how "The Lord took a form and that was a divided form, half woman, and half man. On one side, beautiful garlands : on the other, bone ear-rings, and coils of snakes. On one side the hair black, beautiful, and in curls—on the other, twisted like rope." And then passing immediately into the other form of the same thought, he quoted—

"God became Krishna and Râdhâ—
Love flows in thousands of coils.

Whoso wants, takes it.
Love flows in thousands of coils—
The tide of love and loving past,
And fills the soul with bliss and joy !"

So absorbed was he that his breakfast stood unheeded long after it was ready, and when at last he went reluctantly,—saying 'When one has all this *bhakti* what does one want with food?'—it was only to come back again quickly, and resume the subject.

But, either now or at some other time, he said that he did not talk of Râdhâ and Krishna, where he looked for deeds. It was Siva who made stern and earnest workers, and to Him the labourer must be dedicated.

The next day, he gave us a quaint saying of Sri Râmakrishna, comparing the critics of others to bees or flies, according as they chose honey or wounds.

And then we were off to Islamabad, and really, as it proved, to Amarnâth.

*July 19th.*

The first afternoon, in a wood by the side of the Jhelum, we discovered the long-sought

Temple of Pandrenthan (Pandresthan, place of the Pandavas?)

It was sunk in a pond, and this was thickly covered with scum, out of which it rose, a tiny cathedral of the long ago, built of heavy grey limestone. The temple consisted of a small cell, with four doorways, opening to the cardinal points. Externally, it was a tapering pyramid, —with its top truncated, to give foothold to a bush—supported on a four-pierced pedestal. In its architecture, trefoil and triangular arches were combined, in an unusual fashion, with each other, and with the straight-lined lintel. It was built with marvellous solidity, and the necessary lines were somewhat obscured by heavy ornament.

We were all much distressed, on arriving at the edge of the pond in the wood, to be unable to go inside the little temple, and examine the interior decorations, which a number of guide-books declared to be "quite classical," that is to say, Greek or Roman, in form and finish!

Our grief was turned into joy, however, when our *hajjis*, or boatmen, brought up a countryman, who undertook to provide a boat for us. This he brought out, *from under the scum*, and placing a chain on it, he proceeded to drag us each in turn about the lake, himself wading almost waist-deep in the water. So we were able, as we had desired, to go inside.

For all but the Swami himself, this was our first peep at Indian archæology. So when he had been through it, he taught us how to observe the interior.

In the centre of the ceiling was a large sun-medallion, set in a square whose points were the points of the compass. This left four equal triangles, at the corners of the ceiling, which were filled with sculpture in low relief, male and female figures intertwined with serpents, beautifully done. On the wall were empty spaces, where seemed to have been a band of topes.

Outside, carvings were similarly distributed. In one of the trefoil arches—over, I think, the eastern door,—was a fine image of the Teaching Buddha, standing, with His hand uplifted. Running round the buttresses was a much-defaced frieze of a seated woman, with a tree,—evidently Mâyâ Devi, the Mother of Buddha.

The three other door-niches were empty, but a slab by the pond-side seemed to have fallen from one, and this contained a bad figure of a king, said by the country-people to represent the sun. The masonry of this little temple was superb, and probably accounted for its long preservation. A single block of stone would be so cut as to correspond, not to one brick in a wall, but to a section of the architect's plan. It would turn a corner and form part of two distinct walls, or sometimes even of three. This fact made one take the building as very, very old, possibly even earlier than Marttanda. The theory of the workmen seemed so much more that of carpentering than of building! The water about it, was probably an overflow, into the temple-court, from the sacred spring that the chapel itself may have been placed, as the Swami thought, to enshrine.

To him, the place was delightfully suggestive. It was a direct memorial of Buddhism, representing one of the four religious periods into which he had already divided the History of Kashmir :

(1) Tree and Snake-worship, from which

dated all the names of the springs ending in Nâg, as Vêrnâg, and so on; (2) Buddhism; (3) Hinduism, in the form of Sun-worship; and (4) Mohammedanism. Sculpture, he told us, was the characteristic art of Buddhism, and the sun-medallion, or lotus, one of its commonest ornaments. The figures with the serpents referred to pre-Buddhism. But sculpture had greatly deteriorated under Sun-worship, hence the crudity of the Surya figure.

And then we left the little temple in the woods. What had it held, that men might worship, nearly eighteen centuries ago,* when the world was big, with the births of mighty things? We could not tell. We could only guess. Meanwhile, to one thing we could bow the knee,—the Teaching Buddha. One picture we could conjure up—the great wood-built city, with this at its heart, long years afterwards destroyed by fire, and now moved some five miles away. And so, with a dream and a sigh,

* We assumed Pandrenthan, when we saw it, to be of Kaniksha's time, 150 A. D.—I am not sure that it is really so old —N.

we wended our way back through the trees, to the river-side.

It was the time of sunset,—such a sunset! The mountains in the west were all a shimmering purple. Further north, they were blue with snow and cloud. The sky was green and yellow and touched with red,—bright flame and daffodil colours, against a blue and opal background. We stood and looked, and then the Master, catching sight of the throne of Solomon —that little Takt which we already loved—exclaimed "what genius the Hindu shows in placing his temples! He always chooses a grand scenic effect! See! The Takt commands the whole of Kashmir. The rock of Hari Parbat rises red out of blue water, like a lion couchant, crowned. And the Temple of Marttanda has the valley at its feet!"

Our boats were moored near the edge of the wood, and we could see that the presence of the silent chapel, of the Buddha, which we had just explored, moved the Swami deeply. That evening we all foregathered in *Dhirâ Mâtâ*'s houseboat, and a little of the conversation has been noted down.

Our Master had been talking of Christian ritual as derived from Buddhist, but one of the party would have none of the theory.

"Where did Buddhist ritual itself come from?" She asked.

"From Vedic," answered the Swami briefly.

"Or as it was present also in southern Europe, is it not better to suppose a common origin for it, and the Christian, and the Vedic rituals?"

"No! No!" he replied. "You forget that Buddhism was entirely within Hinduism! Even caste was not attacked—it was not yet crystallised, of course!—and Buddha merely tried to restore the ideal. *He who attains to God in this life*, says Manu, *is the Brahmin*. Buddha would have had it so, if he could."

"But how are Vedic and Christian rituals connected?" persisted his opponent. "How *could* they be the same? You have nothing even corresponding to the central rite of our worship!"

"Why yes!" said the Swami, "Vedic ritual has its Mass, the offering of food to God, your Blessed Sacrament, our *prasâdam*. Only it is offered sitting, not kneeling, as is common in hot countries. They kneel in Tibet. Then, too, Vedic ritual has its lights, incense, music."

"But", was the somewhat ungracious argument, "has it any common prayer?" Objections urged in this way always elicited some bold paradox which contained a new and unthought-of generalisation.

He flashed down on the question. "No! and neither had christianity! That is pure protestantism and protestantism took it from the Mohammedans, perhaps through Moorish influence!

"Mohammedanism is the only religion that has completely broken down the idea of the priest. The leader of prayer stands with his back to the people, and only the reading of the Koran may take place from the pulpit. Protestantism is an approach to this.

"Even the tonsure existed in India, in the shaven head. I have seen a picture of Justinian receiving the Law from two monks, in which the monks' heads are entirely shaven. The monk and nun both existed, in pre-Buddhistic

Hinduism. Europe gets her orders from the Thebaid."

"At that rate, then, you accept Catholic ritual as Aryan!"

"Yes almost all Christianity is Aryan, I believe. I am inclined to think Christ never existed. I have doubted that, ever since I had my dream,—that dream off Crete!* Indian and Egyptian ideas met at Alexandria, and went forth to the world, tinctured with Judaism and Hellenism, as Christianity.

"The Acts and Epistles, you know, are older than the Gospels, and S. John is spurious. The only figure we can be sure of is S. Paul, and he was not an eye-witness, and according to his own showing was capable of Jesuitry—"by all means save souls"—isn't it?

* In travelling from Naples to Port Said, on his way back to India, in January 1897, the Swami had a dream of an old and bearded man, who appeared before him, saying "This is the island of Crete," and showing him a place in the island, that he might afterwards identify. The vision went to say that the religion of Christianity had originated in the island of Crete and in connection with this gave him two European words,—one of which was *Therapeutæ*—which it declared, were derived from

"No! Buddha and Mahommed, alone amongst religious teachers, stand out with historic distinctness,—having been fortunate enough to have, while they were living, enemies as well as friends. Krishna—I doubt; a yogi, and a

---

Sanskrit. *Therapeutæ* meant sons (from the Sanskrit *putra*) of the Theras, or Buddhist monks. From this the Swami was to understand that Christianity had originated in a Buddhist mission. The old man added "The proofs are all here," pointing to the ground. "Dig and you will see!"

As he awoke, feeling that this was no common dream, the Swami rose, and tumbled out on deck. Here he met an officer, turning in from his watch. "What o'clock is it?—said the Swami. "Mid-night!"—was the answer. "Where are we?"—he then said; when, to his astonishment, the answer came back—"fify miles off Crete!"

Our Master used to laugh at himself for the strength of the impression that this dream had made on him. But he could never shake it off. The fact that the second of the two etymologies has been lost, is deeply to be regretted. The Swami had to say that before he had had this dream, it had never occurred to him to doubt that the personality of Christ was strictly historic. We must remember, however, that according to Hindu philosophy, it is the completeness of an idea that is important, and not the question of its historical authenticity. The Swami once asked Sri Râmakrishna, when he was a boy, about this very matter. "Don't you think!" answered his Guru, "that those who could invent such things were themselves that?"

shepherd, and a great king, have all been amalgamated in one beautiful figure, holding the Gitâ in his hand.

"Renan's life of Jesus is mere froth. It does not touch Strauss, the real antiquarian. Two things stand out as personal living touches in the life of Christ,—the woman taken in adultery,—the most beautiful story in literature,—and the woman at the well. How strangely true is this last, to Indian life! A woman, coming to draw water, finds, seated at the well-side, a yellow-clad monk. He asks her for water. Then He teaches her, and does a little mind-reading and so on. Only in an Indian story, when she went to call the villagers, to look and listen, the monk would have taken his chance, and fled to the forest!

"On the whole, I think old Rabbi Hillel is responsible for the teachings of Jesus, and an obscure Jewish sect of Nazarenes—a sect of great antiquity—suddenly galvanised by S. Paul, furnished the mythic personality, as a centre of worship.

"The Resurrection, of course, is simply spring-cremation. Only the rich Greeks and

Romans had had cremation any way, and the new sun-myth would only stop it amongst the few.

"But Buddha! Buddha! Surely he was the greatest man who ever lived. He never drew a breath for himself. Above all, he never claimed worship. He said, "Buddha is not a man, but a state. I have found the door. Enter, all of you!"

"He went to the feast of Ambâpâli, 'the sinner.' He dined with the pariah, though he knew it would kill him, and sent a message to his host on his death-bed, thanking him for the great deliverance. Full of love and pity for a little goat, even before he had attained the truth! You remember how he offered his own head, that of prince and monk, if only the king would spare the kid that he was about to sacrifice and how the king was struck by his compassion, that he saved its life? Such a mixture of rationalism and feeling was never seen! Surely, surely, there was none like him!"

# CHAPTER IX.

## WALKS AND TALKS BESIDE THE JHELLUM.

*Persons* :—The Swami Vivekananda, and a party of Europeans, amongst whom were Dhirâ Mâtâ, the 'Steady Mother' ; 'One whose name was Jayâ' ; and Niveditâ.
*Place* :—Kashmir.
*Time* :—July 20th to July 29th, 1898.

### *July 20th.*

Next day, we came to the ruins of the two great temples of Avantipur. Each hour, as we went deeper and deeper into the interior, the river and the mountains grew more lovely. And amidst the immediate attractions of fields and trees, and people with whom we felt thoroughly at home, how difficult it was to remember that we were exploring a stream in Central Asia! To those who have seen Kashmir in any season, a wealth of memory is called up, by Kalidas picture of the spring-forest, in all its beauty of wild cherry-blossom, and almond and apple,—

that forest, in which Siva sits beneath a deodar, when Umâ, princess of the Himalaya, enters with her offering of a lotus-seed garland, while close at hand stands the beautiful young god with his quiver and bow of flowers. All that is divine in an English spring, or lovely in the woods of Normandy, at Eastertide, is gathered up and multiplied, in the charms of the vale of Kashmir.

That morning, the river was broad and shallow and clear, and two of us walked with the Swami, across the fields and along the banks, about three miles. He began by talking of the sense of sin, how it was Egyptian, Semitic and Aryan. It appears in the Vedas, but quickly passes out. The Devil is recognised there, as the Lord of Anger. Then, with the Buddhists, he became Mâra, the Lord of Lust, and one of the most loved of the Lord Buddha's titles was "conqueror of Mâra," *vide* the Sanskrit lexicon (Amarkosha) that Swami learnt to patter, as a child of four! But while Satan is the Hamlet of the Bible, in the Hindu scriptures, the Lord of Anger never divides creation. He always represents defilement, never duality.

Zoroaster was a reformer of some old religion. Even Ormuzd and Ahriman, with him, were not supreme : they were only manifestations of the Supreme. That order religion must have been Vedantic. So the Egyptians and Semites cling to the theory of sin, while the Aryans, as Indians and Greeks, quickly lose it. In India, righteousness and sin become *vidyâ* and *avidyâ*, —both to be transcended. Amongst the Aryans, Persians and Europeans become Semitised, by religious ideas, hence the sense of sin.*

And then the talk drifted, as it was always so apt to do, to questions of the country and the future. What idea must be urged on a people, to give them strength? The line of their own development runs in one way, A. Must the new accession of force be a compensating one, B? This would produce a development midway between the two, C, a geometrical alteration, merely. But it was not so. National life

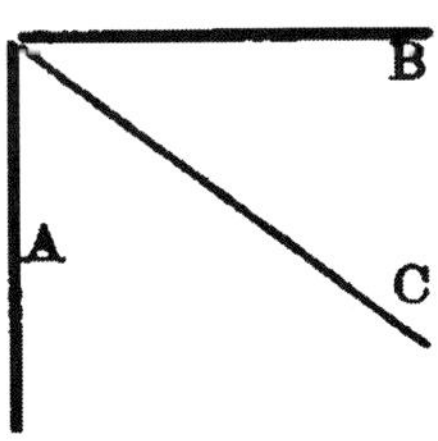


* One of those who listened to this talk, had a wonderful opportunity, later, of appreciating the accuracy, as well as the breadth of the Swami's knowledge,

was a question of organic forces. We must reinforce the current of that life itself, and leave it to do the rest. Buddha preached renunciation, and India heard. Yet within a thousand years, she had reached her highest point of national prosperity. The national life in India has renunciation as its source. Its highest ideals are service and *mukti*. The Hindu mother eats last. Marriage is not for individual happiness, but for the welfare of the nation and the caste. Certain individuals of the modern reform, having embarked on an experiment which could not solve the problem, "are the sacrifices, over which the race has to walk."

And then the trend of conversation changed again, and became all fun and merriment, jokes and stories. And as we laughed and listened, the boats came up, and talk was over for the day.

The whole of that afternoon and night, the Swami lay in his boat, ill. But next day, when we landed at the temple of Bijbehâra—already

---

when she saw two Parsis glad to sit at his feet, and learn from him the history of their own religious ideas.—N.

thronged with Amarnâth pilgrims—he was able to join us for a little while. "Quickly up and quickly down," as he said of himself, was always his characteristic. After that, he was with us most of the day, and in the afternoon, we reached Islamabad.

The *dungas* were moored beside an apple-orchard. Grass grew down to the water's edge, and dotted over the lawn stood the apple and pear and even plum trees, that a Hindu state used to think it necessary to plant, outside each village. In spring-time, it seemed to us, this spot must be that very Island-Valley of Avilion.

"Where falls not hail, or rain, or any snow.
Nor ever wind blows loudly; but it lies,
Deep-meadowed, happy, fair with orchard-lawns,
And bowery hollows, crowned with summer sea."

The houseboat, in which two of us lived, could not be taken so far, so it came to rest in a very deep and rapid portion of the stream, between high hedges, and how beautiful was the walk, from the one point to the other, under the avenue of poplars, with the wonderful green of young rice on either hand !

In the dusk that evening, one came into the little group amongst the apple trees, and found the Master engaged in the rarest of rare happenings, a personal talk with *Dhirâ Mâtâ,* and her whose name was Jayâ. He had taken two pebbles into his hand, and was saying how, when he was well, his mind might direct itself to this and that, or his will might seem less firm, but let the least touch of pain or illness come, let him look death in the face for a while, and "I am as hard as that (knocking the stones together), for I *have* touched the feet of God." And one remembered, *apropos* of this coolness, the story of a walk across the fields, in England, where he and an Englishman and woman had been pursued by an angry bull. The Englishman frankly ran, and reached the other side of the hill in safety. The woman ran as far as she could, and then sank to the ground, incapable of further effort. Seeing this, and unable to aid her, the Swami,—thinking "So *this* is the end, after all"—took up his stand in front of her, with folded arms. He told afterwards how his mind was occupied with a mathematical calculation, as to how far the bull would be able to throw. But the animal suddenly stopped, a few paces off, and then, raising his head, retreated sullenly.

A like courage—though he himself was far from thinking of these incidents—had shown itself, in his early youth, when he quietly stepped up to a runaway horse, and caught it, in the streets of Calcutta, thus saving the life of the woman, who occupied the carriage behind.

The talk drifted on, as we sat on the grass beneath the trees, and became, for an hour or two, half grave, half gay. We heard much of the tricks the monkeys could play, in Brindaban. And we elicited stories of two separate occasions in his wandering life, when he had had clear previsions of help, which had been fulfilled. One of these I remember. It may possibly have occurred at the time when he was under the vow to ask for nothing, and he had been several days (perhaps five) without food. Suddenly, as he lay, almost dying of exhaustion, in a railway-station, it flashed into his mind that he must rise up, and go out along a certain road, and that there he would meet a man, bringing him help.

He obeyed, and met one, carrying a tray of food. "Are you he to whom I was sent?" said this man, coming up to him, and looking at him closely.

Then a child was brought to us, with its hand badly cut, and the Swami applied an old wives' cure. He bathed the wound with water, and then laid on it, to stop the bleeding, the ashes of a piece of calico. The villagers were soothed and consoled, and our gossip was over for the evening.

*July 23rd.*

The next morning, a motley gathering of coolies assembled beneath the apple-trees and waited some hours, to take us to the ruins of Marttanda. It had been a wonderful old building—evidently more abbey than temple,—in a wonderful position, and its great interest lay in the obvious agglomeration of styles and periods in which it had grown up. Never can I forget the deep black shadows under the series of arches that confronted us, as we entered in mid-afternoon, with the sun directly behind us, in the west. There were three arches, one straight behind the other, and just within the farthest of them, at two-thirds of its height, a heavy straight-lined window top. The arches were all trefoil, but only the first and second showed this, as we saw them at the moment of entering. The place had evidently originated as three small rectangular temples, built, with heavy blocks of stone, round sacred springs. The style of these three chambers was all straight-lined, severe. Taking the middle and furthest East of the three, some later king had built round it an enclosing wall, placing a trefoil arch outside each low lintel-formed doorway, without interfering with the original in any way, and then had added to it in front, a larger nave, with a tall trefoil arch as entrance. Each building had been so perfect, and the motive of the two epochs of construction was so clear that the plan of the temple was pure delight, and until one had drawn it, one could not stop. The *dharmsâlâ* or cloister, round the central building, was extraordinarily Gothic in shape, and to one who has seen this, and the royal tombs of Mohammedanism in the north of India, it is at once suggested that the cloister is, ideally, the whole of a monastery, and though, in our cold climates, it can not be so retained, its presence is a perpetual reminder that the East was the original home of monasticism. The Swami was hard at work, in an instant, on observations and theories, pointing out the cornice that ran along the nave from the entrance to the sanctuary, to the west, surmounted by the high trefoils of the two arches and also by a frieze; or showing us the panels containing cherubs; and before we had done, had picked up a of couple coins. The ride back, through the sun-set light, was charming. From all these hours, the day before and the day after, fragments of talk come back to me.

"No nation, not Greek or another, has ever carried patriotism so far as the Japanese. They don't talk, they act—give up all for country. There are noblemen now living in Japan as peasants, having given up their princedoms without a word to create the unity of the empire.* And not one traitor could be found in the Japanese war. Think of that!"

* This is, I think a mistake. It was their political privileges, not their estates, than the Japanese samurais renounced.

Again, talking of the inability of some to express feeling, "Shy and reserved people, I have noticed, are always the most brutal when roused."

Again, evidently talking of the ascetic life, and giving the rules of *brahmacharya*—"The sannyâsin who thinks of gold, to desire it, commits suicide", and so on.

*July 24th.*

The darkness of night and the forest, a great pinefire under the trees, two or three tents standing out white in the blackness, the forms and voices of many servants at their fires in the distance, and the Master with three disciples, such is the next picture. Of the road to Vêr-nâg, under the apple-orchards and along the common-sides, of the pouring rain, and the luncheon in the hard-won sunshine, of that grand old palace of Jehangir, with its octagonal tank at the foot of the pine-wooded hills, much might be said. But the crown of the day came in the hours after dinner, when we were, at long last, alone, and the constant file of visitors and worshippers, with their gifts, had ceased.

Suddenly the Master turned to one member of the party and said "You never mention your school now, do you sometimes forget it? You see," he went on, "I have much to think of. One day I turn to Madras, and think of the work there. Another day I give all my attention to America or England or Ceylon or Calcutta. Now I am thinking about yours."

At that moment the Master was called away to dine, and not till he came back could the confidence he had invited, be given.

He listened to it all, the deliberate wish for a tentative plan, for smallness of beginnings, and the final inclination to turn away from the idea of inclusiveness and breadth, and to base the whole of an educational effort on the religious life, and on the worship of Sri Râmakrishna.

"Because you must be sectarian to get that enthusiasm, must you not?" he said. "You will make a sect in order to rise above all sects. Yes I understand."

There would be obvious difficulties. The thing sounded, on this scale, almost impossible, for many reasons. But for the moment the only care need be to will rightly, and if the plan was sound, ways and means would be found to hand, that was sure.

He waited a little when he had heard it all, and then he said, "You ask me to criticise, but that I cannot do. For I regard you as inspired, quite as much inspired as I am. You know that's the difference between other religions and us. Other people believe their founder was inspired, and so do we. But so am I, also, just as much so as he, and you as I, and after you, your girls and their disciples will be. So I shall help you to do what you think best."

Then he turned to Dhirâ Mâtâ and to Jayá, and spoke of the greatness of the trust that he would leave in the hands of that disciple who should represent the interests of women, when he should go west, of how it would exceed the responsibility of work for men. And he added, turning to the worker of the party, "Yes, you have faith, but you have not that burning enthusiasm that you need. You want to be consumed energy. Siva! Siva!"—and so, invoking the blessing of Mahâdeva, he said goodnight and left us, and we, presently, went to bed.

*July 25th.*

The next morning, we breakfasted early, in one of the tents, and went on to Achhabal. One of us had had a dream of old jewels lost and restored, all bright and new. But the Swami, smiling, stopped the tale, saying "Never talk of a dream as good as that!"

At Achhabal, we found more gardens of Jehangir. Was it here, or at Vêrnâg, that had been his favourite resting-place?

We roamed about the gardens, and bathed in a still pool opposite the Pathan Khan's Zenana, and then we lunched in the first garden, and rode down in the afternoon to Islamabad.

As we sat at lunch, the Swami invited his daughter to go to the Cave of Amarnâth with him, and be dedicated to Siva. Dhirâ Mâtâ smiled permission, and the next half-hour was given to pleasure and congratulations. It had already been arranged that we were all to go to Pahlgaon and wait there for the Swami's return from the pilgrimage. So we reached the boats that evening, packed, and wrote letters, and next day in the afternoon, started for Bawan.

---

# CHAPTER X

## THE SHRINE OF AMARNATH.

*Time* :—July 29th to August 8th 1898.
*Place* :—Kashmir.

*July 29th.*

From this time we saw very little of the Swami. He was full of enthusiasm about the pilgrimage and lived mostly on one meal a day, seeking no company much, save that of *sâdhus*. Sometimes he would come to a camping-ground, beads in hand. To-night two of the party went roaming about Bawan, which was like a village fair, all modified by a religious tendency, centering in the sacred springs. Afterwards, with Dhirâ Mâtâ it was possible to go and listen, at the tent door, to the crowd of Hindi-speaking *sâdhus* who were plying the Swami with questions.

On Thursday, we reached Pahlgaon, and camped down at the lower end of the valley.

We found that the Swami had to encounter high opposition over the question of our admission at all. He was supported by the Naked Swamis, one of whom said, "It is true you have this strength, Swamiji, but you ought not to manifest it!" He yielded at the word. That afternoon however, he took his daughter round the camp to be blessed, which really meant to distribute alms,—and whether because he was looked upon as rich, or because he was recognised as strong the next day our tents were moved up to a lovely knoll, at the head of the camp, where we had the rushing Lidar in front of us, and pine-covered mountains opposite, with a glacier distinctly visible, beyond a cleft high up. We stayed a whole day, at this village, of the shepherds, to keep *ekâdasi*, and early next morning the pilgrims left.

*July 30th.*

At six in the morning we had breakfasted and were off. What time the camp had moved, it seemed impossible to guess, for even at our early meal-time very few pilgrims or tents were left. The ashes of dead fires were all that marked the place where yesterday had been a thousand people and their canvas homes.

How beautiful was the route to the next halt, Chandanawara! There we camped on the edge of a ravine. It rained all afternoon, and I was visited by the Swami only for a five-minute's chat. But I received endless touching little kindnesses from the servants and other pilgrims. In the interval between two showers I went out botanising, and found seven or eight species of *Myesotis*, two of which were new to me. Then I went back to the shadow of my dripping fir-tree.

The second stage was much harder than any of the others. It seemed endless. Close to Chandanawara, the Swami insisted on my doing my first glacier on foot, and took care to point out every detail of interest. A tremendous climb of some thousands of feet, was the next experience. Then a long walk along a narrow path that twisted round mountain after mountain, and finally another steep climb. At the top of the first mountain, the ground was simply carpeted with edelwiess. Then the road passed five hundred feet above Shisharnag, with its sulky water, and at last we camped in a cold damp place amongst the snow-peaks, 18,000 feet high. The firs were far below, and all afternoon and evening the coolies had to forage for juniper in all directions. The Tahsildar's, Swami's and my own tents were all close together, and in the evening a large fire was lighted in front. But it did not burn well, and many feet below lay the glacier. I did not see the Swami after we camped.

Pantajharni—the place of the five streams—was not nearly such a long march. Moreover, it was lower than Shisharnag, and the cold was dry and exhilarating. In front of the camp was a dry river-bed, all gravel, and through this ran five streams, in all which it was the duty of the pilgrim to bathe, walking from one to the other in wet garments. Contriving to elude observation completely, Swamiji nevertheless fulfilled the law to the last letter in this respect.

How lovely were the flowers! The night before, or was it this night? large blue and white anemones grew in my tent, beneath my bed! And here, wandering off, in the afternoon, to see a glacier at closer quarters, I found gentian, sedums, saxifrages, and a new forget-me-not with little hairy silver leaves, thick like velvet pile. Even of juniper at this place there was very little.

At these heights we often found ourselves in great circles of snow-peaks, those mute giants that have suggested to the Hindu mind the idea of the Ash-encovered God.

*August 2nd.*

On Tuesday, August the 2nd, the great day of Amarnâth, the first batch of pilgrims must have left the camp at two! We left by the light of the full moon. The sun rose as we went down the narrow valley. It was not too safe, at this part of the journey. But when we left our *dândies* and began to climb, the real danger began. A sort of goat-path in almost vertical hill-sides, becoming in the descent on the other side, a tiny staircase in the turf. Every here and there, delicate columbines, Michaelmas daisies, and wild roses, tempted one to risk life and limb in their acquisition. Then, having at last reached the bottom of the farther slope, we had to toil along the glacier, mile after mile, to the Cave. About a mile before our destination, the ice ceased, and in the flowing water the pilgrims had to bathe. Even when we seemed to have arrived, there was still quite a stiff ascent over the rocks to be made.

The Swami, exhausted, had by this time, fallen behind, but I, not remembering that he might be ill, waited, below the banks of gravel for his appearance. He came at last, and, with a word, sent me on, he was going to bathe. Half an hour later he entered the cave. With a smile he knelt, first at one end of the semi-circle, then at the other. The place was vast, large enough to hold a cathedral, and the great ice-Siva, in a niche of deepest shadow, seemed as if throned on its own base. A few minutes passed, and then he turned to leave the cave.

To him, the heavens had opened. He had touched the feet of Siva. He had had to hold himself tight, he said afterwards, lest he 'should swoon away.' But so great was his physical exhaustion, that a doctor said afterwards that his heart ought to have stopped beating, and had undergone a permanent enlargement instead.

How strangely near fulfilment had been those words of his Master, "when he realises who and what he is he will give up this body!"

"I have enjoyed it so much!" he said half an hour afterwards, as he sat on a rock above the stream-side, eating lunch with the kind Naked Swami and myself. "I thought the ice-lingam was Siva Himself. And there were no thievish Brahmins, no trade, nothing wrong. It was all worship. I never enjoyed any religious place so much!"

Afterwards he would often tell of the overwhelming vision that had seemed to draw him almost into its vertex. He would talk of the poetry of the white ice-pillar, and it was he who suggested that the first discovery of the place had been by a party of shepherds, who had wandered far in search of their flocks one summer day, and had entered the cave to find themselves, before the unmelting ice, in the presence of the Lord Himself. He always said too that the grace of Amarnâth had been granted to him there, not to die till he himself should give consent. And to me he said "You do not now understand. But you have made the pilgrimage, and it will go on working. Causes must bring their effects. You will understand better afterwards. The effects will come."

How beautiful was the road by which we returned next morning Pahlgaon; We struck tents that night immediately on our return to them, and camped later for the night in a snowy pass a whole stage further on. We paid a coolie a few annas here, to push on with a letter, but when we actually arrived next afternoon we found that this had been quite unnecessary, for all morning long, relays of pilgrims had been passing the tents, and dropping in, in the most friendly manner, to give the others news of us, and our impending arrival. In the morning, we were up and on the way long before dawn. As the sun rose before us, while the moon went down behind, we passed above the Lake of Death, into which about forty pilgrims had been hurried one year, by an avalanche which their hymns had started. After this we came to the tiny goat-path down the face of a steep cliff, by which we were able to shorten the return journey so much. This was little better than a scramble, and everyone had perforce to do it on foot. At the bottom, the villagers had something like breakfast ready. Fires were burning, *chapatties* baking, and tea ready to be served out. From this time on, parties of pilgrims would leave the main body at each parting of the ways, and the feeling of solidarity that had grown up amongst us all throughout the journey became gradually less and less.

That evening in the knoll above Pahlgaon, when a great fire of pine-logs was lighted, and *dhurries* spread we all sat and talked. Our friend, the Naked Swami, joined us and we had plenty of fun and nonsense, but presently, when all had gone save our own little party, we sat on, with the great moon overhead, and the towering snows, and rushing river, and the mountain-pines. And the Swami talked of Siva, and the Cave and the great verge of vision.

*August 8th.*

We started for Islamabad next day, and on Monday morning as we sat at breakfast, we were towed safely into Srinagar.

# CHAPTER XI

## AT SRINAGAR ON THE RETURN JOURNEY.

*Persons* :—The Swami Vivekananda, and a party of Europeans, amongst whom were Dhirâ Mâtâ, the 'Steady Mother.' 'One whose name was Jayâ' ; and Niveditâ.

*Place* :—Kashmir—Srinagar.

*Time* :—August 9th to August 13th.

*August 9th.*

At this time the Master was always talking of leaving us. And when I find the entry "The River is pure that flows, the monk is pure that goes," I know exactly what it means—the passionate outcry "I am always so much better when I have to undergo hardships and beg my bread," the longing for freedom and the touch of the common people, the picture of himself making a long circuit of the country on foot, and meeting us again at Baramulla for the journey home.

His family of boat-people, whom he had

staunchly befriended through two seasons, left us to-day. Afterwards he would refer to the whole incident of their connection with him as proof that even charity and patience could go too far.

*August 10th.*

It was evening, and we all went out to pay some visit. On the return he called his disciple Niveditâ to walk with him arross the fields. His talk was all about the work and his intentions in it. He spoke of the inclusiveness of his conception of the country and its religions; of his own distinction as being solely in his desire to make Hinduism active, aggressive, a missionary faith; of 'dont-touch-ism' as the only thing he repudiated. Then he talked with depth of feeling of the gigantic spirituality of many of those who were most orthodox. India wanted practically, but she must never let go her hold on the old meditative life for that. "To be as deep as the ocean and as broad as the Sky" —Sri Râmakrishna has said, was the ideal. But this profound inner life in the soul encased within orthodoxy, is the result of an accidental not an essential association. "And if we set ourselves right here, the world will be right, for are we not all one?" Râmakrishna Paramahamsa was alive to the depths of his being, yet on the outer plane he was perfectly active and capable."

And then of that critical question of the worship of his own Master, "My own life is guided by the enthusiasm, of that great personality, but others will decide for themselves how far this is true for them. Inspiration is not filtered out to the world through one man."

*August 11th.*

There was occasion this day for the Swami to rebuke a member of this party for practising palmistry. It was a thing he said that everyone desired, yet all India despised and hated. Yes, he said, in reply to a little special pleading, even of character-reading he disapproved. "To tell you the truth I should have thought even your Incarnation more honest if He and His disciples had not performed miracles. Buddha unfrocked a monk for doing it." Later, talking on the subject to which he had now transferred his attention, he spoke with horror of the display of the least of it as sure to bring a terrible reflex.

*August 12th and 13th.*

The Swami had now taken a Brâhmin cook. Very touching had been the arguments of the Amarnâth *sâdhus* against his willingness to let even a Mussalmán cook for him. "Not in the land of Sikhs, at least Swamiji" : they had said, and he had at last consented. But for the present he was worshipping his little Mohammedan boat-child as Umâ. Her whole idea of love was service, and the day he left Kashmir, she, tiny one, was fain to carry a tray of apples for him all the way to the tonga herself. He never forget her, though he seemed quite indifferent at the time. In Kashmir itself he was fond of recalling the time when she saw a blue flower on the towing path and sitting down before it, and striking it this way and that, "was alone with that flower for twenty minutes."

There was a piece of land by the river-side on which grew three chennaars, towards which our thoughts turned with peculiar love at this time. For the Maharajah was anxious to give it to Swamiji, and we all pictured it as a centre of work in the future-work which should realise the great idea of "by the people, for the people, as a joy to worker and to served."

In view of Indian feeling about a homestead blessed by women, it had been suggested that we should go and annex the site, by camping there for a while. One of our party moreover had a personal wish for special quiet at this time. So it was decided that we should establish 'a women's math', as it were, before the Maharajah should require the land, to confer it on the Swami. And this was possible because the spot was one of the minor camping grounds used by Europeans.

# CHAPTER XII

## The Camp under the Chennaars.

*Persons* :—The Swami Vivekananda, and a party of Europeans, amongst whom were Dhirâ Mâtâ, the 'Steady Mother.' 'One whose name was Jayâ' ; and Niveditâ.

*Place* :—Kashmir—Srinagar.

*Time* :—August 14th to September 20th.

### *August 14th to Sept. 3rd.*

It was Sunday morning and next afternoon the Swami was prevailed on to come up to tea with us, in order to meet a European guest, who seemed to be interested in the subject of Vedânta. He had been little inclined to concern himself with the matter, and I think his real motive in accepting, was probably to afford his too-eager disciples an opportunity of convincing themselves of the utter futility of all such attempts as this. Certainly he took infinite pains with the enquirer and as certainly his trouble was wasted. I remember his saying, amongst other things, "How I wish a law could be broken. If we were really able to break a law we should be free. What you call breaking the law, is really only another way of keeping it." Then he tried to explain a little of the super-conscious life. But his words fell on ears that could not hear.

*September 16th.*

On Tuesday he came once more to our little camp to the mid-day meal. Towards the end, it began to rain heavily enough to prevent his return, and he took up Tod's "History of Rajasthan" which was lying near, and drifted into talk of Meerâ Bâi. "Two-thirds of the national ideas now in Bengal," he said, "have been gathered from this book." But the episode of Meerâ Bâi, the queen who would not be queen, but would wander the world with the lovers of Krishna, was always his favourite, even in Tod. He talked of how she preached submission, prayerfulness, and service to all in contrast to Chaitanya, who preached love to the Name of God, and mercy to all. Meerâ Bâi was always one of his great patronesses. He would put into her story many threads with which one is now familiar in other connections, such as the conversion of two great robbers, and the end by an image of Krishna opening and swallowing her up. I heard him on one occasion recite and translate one of her songs to a woman. I wish I could remember the whole, but it began, in his rendering, with the words, "Cling to it, cling to it, cling to it, Brother," and ended with "If Aunkâ and Bunkâ—the robber brothers, Sujana—the fell butcher, and the courtesan, who playfully taught her parrot to repeat the name of the Lord Krishna were saved, there is hope for all." Again I have heard him tell that marvellous tale of Meerâ Bâi, in which on reaching Brindâvana, she sent for a certain famous *sâdhu*.* He refused to go, on the ground that woman might not see men in Brindâvana. When this had happened three times, Meerâ Bâi went to him herself saying that she had not known that there were such beings as men there, she had supposed that

* Sanâtana, the famous Sannyasin disciple of Sri Chaitanya of Bengal, who gave up his office of minister to the Nawab of Bengal to become a religious devotee.

Krishna alone existed. And when she saw the astonished *sâdhu* she unveiled herself completely, with the words "Fool, do you call yourself a Man?" And as he fell prostrate before her with a cry of awe, she blessed him as a mother blesses her child.

To-day the Swami passed on to the talk of Akbar, and sang us a song of Tâna Sena, the poet-laureate of the Emperor—

"Seated on the throne, a god amongst men,
Thou the Emperor of Delhi :
Blessed was the hour the minute, the second,
When thou ascendest the throne,
O God amongst men,
Thou the Lord of Delhi.
Long live thy crown, thy sceptre, thy throne,
O God amongst men,
Thou Emperor of Delhi :
Live long, and remain awakened always,
O son of Humayoon,
Joy of the sun, God amongst men,
Thou, the Emperor of Delhi!"

Then the talk passed to "our national hero" Pratâp Singh, who never could be brought to submission. Once indeed he was tempted to give in, at that moment when, having fled from Cheetore, and the queen herself having cooked the scanty evening meal, a hungry cat swooped down on that cake of bread which was the children's portion, and the King of Mewar heard his babies cry for food. Then, indeed, the strong heart of the man failed him. The prospect of ease and relief tempted him. And for a moment he thought of ceasing from the unequal conflict, and sending his alliance to Akbar, only for an instant. The Eternal Will protects its own. Even as the picture passed before his mind, there appeared a messenger, with those despatches from a famous Rajput chief, that said "There is but one left amongst us who has kept his blood free from admixture with the alien. Let it never be said that his head has touched the dust." And the soul of Pratâp drew in the long breath of courage and renewed faith, and he arose and swept the country of its foes, and made his own way back to Oodeypore.

Then there was the wonderful tale of the virgin princess Krishna Kumâri, whose hand was sought by various royal suitors at once. And when three armies were at the gate, her father could think of nothing better than to give her poison. The task was entrusted to her uncle, and he entered her room as she lay asleep to do it. But at the sight of her beauty and youth, remembering her too as a baby, the soldier's heart failed him, and he could not perform his task. But she was awakened by some sound, and being told what was proposed, stretched out her hand for the cup, and drank the poison with a smile. And so on, ant so on. For the stories of Rajput heroes in this kind are endless.

*Sept. 20th.*

On Saturday, the Swami and he whose name was Soong, went to the Dâhl Lake, to be the guests of the American consul and his wife for a couple of days. They returned on Monday, and on Tuesday, the Swami came up to the new Math, as we called it, and had his boat moved close by ours, so that he could be with hs for a few days, before leaving for Ganderbal.

---

## Concluding words of the Editor.

From Ganderbal the Swami returned by the first week of October and announced his intention of leaving for the plains in a few days for urgent reasons. The European party had already made plans to visit the principal cities of Northern India *e.g.* Lahore, Delhi, Agra, etc., as soon as the winter set in. So both parties decided to return together and came to Lahore. From here the Swami and his party returned to Calcutta leaving the rest to carry out their plans for sight-seeing in Northern India.